Make Yourself Indispensable

A Guide for Career Success

Dr. Darren McKnight
Integrity Applications Inc. (IAI)

Roger Campbell
Campbell Consulting Solutions (CCS)

CreateSpace

Make Yourself Indispensable

ISBN-13: 978-1508467557

ISBN-10: 1508467552

Printed in the United States

By CreateSpace

Dedication:

We would like to thank our wives, Alison and Candi, for being truly indispensable in our career successes.

Darren McKnight and Roger Campbell

Make Yourself Indispensable

Table of Contents

Make Yourself Indispensable

I. START YOUR ENGINES

Thank you for reading this book. I know that your time is valuable – it is your most precious asset. If you are reading this book you have taken a deliberate step to improve your chances for career success; we will not waste your time. Just be open to thinking about jobs, employment, and your career differently, then be willing to work hard!

A Little Perspective from Darren McKnight[1]

It is critical to understand that to be truly successful, you must be disciplined and diligent about improving yourself. It seems that no matter how good or bad the economy, it is difficult to gauge just how hard you have to work to stay employed and succeed professionally.

It is simple: work harder than everyone else. Yet, working harder does not necessarily mean working the longest hours. You must combine intelligent, informed thinking and self-assessment in tandem with enlightened, passionate action.

You need to work with purpose and intensity! I hope that you did not think that you could just read a book and re-energize your career without working hard.

> "You must work with purpose and intensity."

---

[1] Darren McKnight is the primary narrator for the book through the first two sections and Roger Campbell takes over for the last two sections.

Make Yourself Indispensable

Are you going to be outsourced or is your organization downsizing? Is your industry shrinking due to global conditions beyond your control and beyond the capacity of your company to respond? Are you just starting a career and trying to make sure that you lay the foundation for a great career? If any of these are true, then this book is for you.

Are you leaving the military or government service after 20-30 years and want to explore the next phase of your career? Are you fifteen years out of college and realizing that your jobs are shaping you rather than you building a career? If yes, then this book is for you! Take the day off tomorrow and finish reading this book now!

Do not wait for events "at the office and beyond" to drive your career development activities. You must act first; let others respond to you. This is the same mantra I use when coaching youth soccer. If you act with purpose, based on deliberate practice, a coherent plan, and passion, you will have the advantage.

> "If you act with purpose, based on deliberate practice, a coherent plan, and passion, you will create a decisive career advantage."

In this book, we will review how to fine-tune your actions so that you will have more opportunities to be successful than you ever imagined.

Make Yourself Indispensable

How often have you looked at the LinkedIn page of a former colleague and asked yourself, "How did he or she get that job"? Reading this book will help you better understand how you can become a person that other people envy as you achieve your own career goals. You cannot sit still; you need to take stock of where you are and what you need to do to move forward.

An old quotation is apt here: "If you enjoy your work then you will never work a day in your life." My children think that I am crazy because I always say that I love my job. However, I really love my career. The fact is that I have done, and continue to do, everything to ensure that I am the pilot of my future. I am not just a passenger on a whitewater raft bouncing from job to job down the rapids of life.

Stop whining about bad luck and focus on your ability to focus; be intense in listening and learning to become indispensable and create career success. It will not just happen.

Why Listen to Us?

How am I qualified to discuss career success? I am not a billionaire, a Nobel Prize winner, or an Olympic standout. I am just a guy with the drive for making the most of the skills with which God has blessed me.

I moved around a lot when I was growing up because my father was in the Marine Corps. I did not attend the same school two years in a row until high school. I went to decent schools in decent locations through high school. I was not the valedictorian but I was a well-balanced student-athlete who enjoyed the pursuit of excellence; I was never the best at anything. That never deterred me; I labored to be *the best that I could be* at everything I did.

When I received a Congressional appointment to the U.S. Air Force Academy, it marked a turning point in my life. I was now a little fish in a big pond with stellar people handpicked from across the United States.

Again, I was not the best at anything but I began to see that being good at many things and being attentive to people who thought and acted differently from me accelerated my career progression and gave me a unique perspective.

I embraced cognitive diversity even before I knew what it meant. What it meant was that I listened to everyone; took note of what worked and what did not work; and then tried to apply the successful approaches in my own life and career.

I learned early that career success was not about finding the right job but crafting an idea of what I wanted as a career and then letting the jobs be waypoints for me navigating that path. Everything I have done to this point is a "work in progress" and not the destination. Everything I have done is both an enabler for the future and also part of my career goal. Success is not a destination; it is a path well-traveled.

> "Success is not a destination; it is a path well-traveled."

Make Yourself Indispensable

I am an active elected member of the International of Academy of Astronautics and have more than 100 publications and presentations in 13 countries. I coauthored the first book ever on artificial space debris while finishing my PhD in Aerospace Engineering Sciences at the University of Colorado in 2.5 years. This space environmental research and analysis to support national and international programs has been a core pillar of my professional career. It is a beachhead that I will support and build on until the day that I die.

However, about a decade into being a world expert in the area of space debris, I decided to focus for five years on a completely different area: chemical and biological (chem/bio) agent modeling, analysis, and decontamination. I developed a concept for applying a commercial technology used for ridding meat and poultry of foodborne pathogens, such as *e-coli* and salmonella, for use by the military to potentially remediate material from chem/bio attacks.

My successful, cooperative research with U.S. government organizations laid the groundwork for the cleaning of tons of mail contaminated in 2001 when the anthrax letters coursed their way through the U.S. Postal Service system.

I returned to space debris research to continue where I had left off but with a renewed appreciation for other approaches and a new set of tools that I could apply. I had also refined my career goal to focus on not only "what" people do to be innovative and productive but also "how" they do it. The "how" can be applied across multiple problem sets and industries and even in your personal life. I started to develop capabilities in industrial energy, infectious disease prediction, metamaterials research, and youth sports training.

> "Success is less about what you do and more about how you do it."

I wrote a soccer coaching book that introduced a new paradigm for youth soccer training. My coauthor, Radovan Pletka, is developing the concepts from this book, *Soccer is a Thinking Game*, into a youth soccer training curriculum that will affect how we use sports to reinforce important life lessons for our youth and encourage them to remain active in sports for a longer period of time. Soccer IS a thinking game - just like making yourself indispensable IS a thinking game. You must balance purposeful thinking with passionate, but deliberate, action.

While continuing my space debris activities, I worked with an enlightened government boss and set of colleagues to establish a program for the development of a predictive awareness framework for infectious disease to enable the warning of deployed U.S. service members. This system provides two weeks warning before the first person gets sick rather than detecting two weeks after the first case (which is the current early warning definition from the World Health Organization). This project was another example of transferring "how" we do things into a new domain.

My industrial energy efforts have resulted in my authorship of a review of renewable energy technologies for a national investment firm and designing a solar-driven pump facility for

Make Yourself Indispensable

the Fish and Wildlife Service to recover lost salt marshes in a critical breeding location for North American aviary. It also landed me as the Chairman of the Board of Advisors for ZF Energy Development (Z-FED).

Why was I asked to help Z-FED? Four years ago, I took the time to contribute to a technical paper on energy arbitrage using my own time on weekends and at night because I was learning and contributing to a domain that I knew was of growing importance. I love to learn and have found that continual learning is a common component of success for any professional who is in high demand (i.e., indispensable).

> "Continual learning is a common component of success for any professional who strives to be indispensable."

Instead of waiting for someone to pay me to do the work, I stuck with my career model of learning about "how" across multiple domains as an enabler to career success. It was painful, hard work that stretched my intellectual and communication skills but I am now reaping the benefits.

I will explain in this book the specific actions and features of a career plan that got me to today and how it can get you more opportunities than you have time. I have "made" time by being efficient, disciplined, and passionate in pursuit of a clear career plan. This process is not about protecting my job; it is about achieving my career aspirations. By the way, it is also not about beating others or defeating adversaries. It is about working cooperatively with purpose and passion.

You determine your future: not your boss, not the economy, not fate, and not your colleagues! More often than not, helping other people along the way may temporarily slow you down but over the long run "paying forward" in business is both personally satisfying and a great investment professionally.

> "Paying forward in business is both personally satisfying and a great investment professionally."

Look at space system survivability, infectious disease outbreak prediction, industrial energy economics, and chem/bio security. I am only trained or formally educated in one of these domains; the rest are the result of passion and persistence. However, I could stop and do any one of these singly as a job right now. That is as close to being indispensable as I think anyone can get.

I love what I am doing and the more I do it, the more options I create. I may indeed stop and take another deep dive into a new area but the diversity of topics with the unity of purpose in examining "how" is still my passion and it creates more opportunities over time!

The First Step

The first step to career success is not to focus on your job but to create a career strategy, which includes how you define success, and then consistently, proactively nurture that strategy. Jobs are not the goal. Decide who you want to be and what you want to stand for. What do you want people to say about you at your funeral? Figure out what verbs and adverbs (not adjectives) would portray your career and characterize your life's accomplishments.

Have an overarching cadence, pace, or tune to your career. Do you want the powerful beat of a marching band or the stirring aria of an opera? Give your career a personality and act consistently to that ideal.

Jobs are like chapters of a book, necessary but not sufficient to tell a story. What is the title of your book? What chapters or jobs will help you build a compelling novel or career?

Innovation as a Core Enabler

The four pillars of innovation, from my book *Hitting The Innovation Jackpot*, reflect critical features of an indispensable person.

Having great communication skills in writing and talking as well as listening and learning are important for anyone hoping to provide value to an organization and achieve success.

Balancing high tech tools and high touch rules creates a linkage to people while ensuring your technical skills do not become dated.

Embracing cognitive diversity allows you to combat the potential psychological inertia of arcane, uncreative organizations.

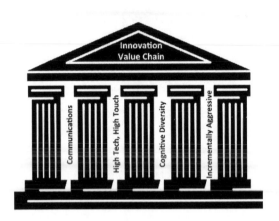

Last, being incrementally aggressive (or assertive) in the implementation of innovations maximizes your chances of breakthrough performance without undue risks.

These are bound together by the innovation value chain that calls for the sequence of communication, cooperation, and collaboration leading to innovation.

Balance comes up often throughout this book. There are pairs such as thinking and acting, high tech and high touch, and tactical and visionary. Diversity in tools and approaches helps you react to a diversity of situations and challenges – and you will have many throughout your career.

Career Success

Despite all of the apparent possibilities, you only have three potential actions when it comes to your career and jobs: get your

Make Yourself Indispensable

first job, improve your career in place, and get a new job (to advance your career).

The primary effort is in enhancing your career in place. Many people want to blame the lack of job satisfaction and career advancement on their current job and the management of the organization for which they work.

In reality, many people change jobs too quickly without investigating how their current work environment can enhance their chances for attaining career success. Do not expect an employer to promote or even manage your career. That is your responsibility.

> "People change jobs too quickly without investigating how their current work environment can enhance their chances for attaining career success."

When I was in the Air Force and we had centralized career advisors. Their job was to allocate resources within the Air Force to benefit the whole organization but not necessarily to advance each individual's career. However, it is important to note now that someone advancing their own career does not have to act counter to what is good for the organization. Employees who think about "careers" rather than "jobs" help the organization.

Having been an executive for a $10B/year company, Science Applications International Corporation, SAIC (http://www.saic.com), I can tell you it is quite refreshing when

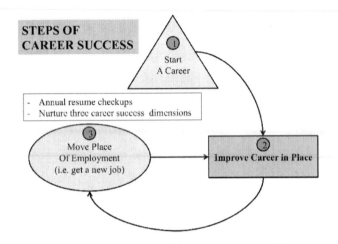

STEPS OF CAREER SUCCESS

① Start A Career

- Annual resume checkups
- Nurture three career success dimensions

③ Move Place Of Employment (i.e. get a new job)

② Improve Career in Place

an employee knows what they want to do with their lives and their careers. The people who have solid careers will also be the ones that organizations will want to keep.

The best career is not created by job-hopping but, rather, by job-leveraging. Manage your career like your individual retirement account; deposit early and often while periodically checking that you are heading in the right direction.

You may need to get a job first or to get a better one, but usually you can advance your career immensely where you are!

To assist in this introspective focus, perform an annual résumé checkup in which you ask "Am I better off this year than I was last year? Have I learned new skills?" If the answer is "no," sit back and figure out the next step in your career: learn a new

16

programming language, get a patent, obtain a certification, or some other specific step.

> "Manage you career like your individual retirement account: deposit early and often while periodically checking that you are heading in the right direction."

Be incrementally assertive. You should attack useful activities in rapid, deliberate succession. Do not blame your organization for your lack of success; take responsibility for your career.

Some people change jobs when it gets tough. It is always better to change a job when you are heading *to* something and not *away* from something. If you do not believe me, then you might believe Earl Nightingale, motivational speaker and author, who said that "the biggest mistake that you can make is to believe you are working for somebody else...the driving force of your career must come from the individual. Remember that jobs are owned by the company, you own your career."

Three years into my job at Titan Corporation, I felt that I was not adding to my skills and accomplishments so I needed to determine how I could add a new dimension to my professional development. I decided that I was weak in intellectual property skills and, to be a better technology executive, I needed expertise in this domain. As a result, I decided to make a new push into patents, trademarks, and copyrights.

Make Yourself Indispensable

This resurgence first took the form of some original research. I focused on applying a commercial technology for killing foodborne pathogens in frozen poultry and hamburger meat to prevent illness from undercooked foods. I hypothesized that this penetrating radiation source, an electron beam, could also remediate material contaminated by a chem/bio agent event.

After a successful test program in concert with several U.S. Government agencies, we published the test results. Less than two months later, the anthrax letters were sent through the U.S. Postal Service system killing several people and contaminating tons of mail and several federal facilities.

As I stated earlier, proactive research paved the way to a multi-million dollar contract and the opportunity to help recover from a national security and public health dilemma.

For two years after that effort, I presented technical briefs all over the world and my activities resulted in several patent applications and one patent issued. My self-analysis and energy applied to a new component of my technical base resulted in a powerful new dimension of my career.

How often do you jumpstart your career by nurturing a new expertise area or developing a unique, marketable skill? By reading this book, you have taken at least one action to accelerate your career progression.

Make Yourself Indispensable

> "How often do you jumpstart your career by nurturing a new expertise area or developing a unique, marketable skill?"

Needed Reinforcements from Roger Campbell

During the drafting of this book it became obvious that this career success guide required some assistance from someone with impeccable credentials in human capital management. Roger Campbell provides his input in the latter portion of this book, the section titled "Getting a New Job."

Roger is a leader and has been a sought-after voice in the human capital and talent management fields for more than forty years. He had a productive career as a human capital officer in the federal government and supported recruitment and staffing operations for one of the most selective government agencies in the world: the Central Intelligence Agency.

As a human capital practitioner in the federal sector and his follow-on career in the private sector, he has applied a unique perspective on what works and what does not work in talent management. He actively coaches individuals on all facets of career planning and career development.

His understanding of the challenges of talent management, from both individual and organizational perspectives makes him attractive to both. He has created successful hiring strategies for organizations and has had notable success helping organizations hire candidates that meet client-specific hiring guidelines through a process he calls precision hiring. His career has included work with Monster.com where he served as a senior consultant to help federal clients improve their hiring into the federal service.

Roger is a graduate of George Mason University located in the suburbs of Washington, D.C. and has many years of experience as a recruiter. He has identified, recruited, and hired hundreds of candidates for both public and private sector organizations. He has reviewed thousands of résumés and is an expert in the talent management field.

He has interviewed and made hiring decisions on applicants for positions from customer service representative to senior executive. Roger has also provided seminars and webinars on topics associated with human capital and is currently a leadership and transition coach. He is a member of the Center for Human Capital Innovation (CHCI, http://centerforhci.org/), a Washington, D.C.-based organization that is helping to move the work in human capital to the forefront of both government and public sector organizations. CHCI recently recognized Roger as one of the top 50 Human Capital Experts in the U.S.

Roger and I first met while serving as officials in support of our local community swim club. Through that community activity, he developed a reputation as someone who could offer advice and guidance in the employment field to adults who were out of work or searching for a new position. Eventually, he was receiving knocks on his door from neighbors with their sons and daughters (mostly recent college graduates) in need of career counseling, résumé writing, and job search strategies. Roger also volunteers to counsel and coach graduating seniors at George Mason University on the art of the job search and how to "win" the interview.

I asked Roger to join me in writing this book to provide his expertise on successfully making a job change: networking, building a compelling résumé, getting the résumé out, winning the interview, and following up from an interview.

Simple...But Not Easy

Before we dive into the three core dimensions of making yourself indispensable I just want to remind the reader that this is a *simple* process but it is *not easy*.

Running a marathon is simple: put one foot in front of the other for 26.2 miles. However, preparing for the race and running the race are not easy. It takes persistence, patience, willingness to give up things at times (such as sleep and recreation), but also finding a balance among the many dimensions of your life.

Dimensions of career success include how you think, how you address problems, how you deal with people, and how you push to be the best without alienating people.

> "How you think, how you attack problems, how you deal with people, and how you push to be the best without alienating people are critical components of career success."

21

Make Yourself Indispensable

A race car is built to run hard and fast, but if its systems are not working together effectively, it won't end up in the winner's circle. Similarly, if you want to take charge of your career and press the gas pedal to the floor, the tools that propel you must be well-crafted and balanced or else they won't run smoothly when you are accelerating toward success.

How hard must you push yourself? A motivational video presentation by Rank Society[2] makes a simple, sobering challenge; "You must want to succeed more than you want to breathe." This implies that it is not easy; nothing beautiful and rewarding comes easily.

> "You must want to succeed more than you want to breathe."

However, if you use the right tools and behave, guided by the right priorities, you will efficiently become indispensable and achieve career success. Most importantly, it will be success as you define it, not how others try to define it for you.

Striving for career success will often not be glamorous at times. The storyline that I use is "who is taking out the trash?" Isn't taking out the trash the last job anybody wants to do? Doesn't it signify your position in the organization if you are taking out the trash? I tell everyone that I mentor or counsel that they must be willing to "take out the trash," to do the least pleasant or most arduous task!

---

[2] https://www.youtube.com/watch?v=xVehWEUdSuk

Make Yourself Indispensable

I tell them to not only be the first to volunteer to "take out the trash" but also to hop up from their chairs with big smiles on their faces, their knees churning high, and clear determination to take out the trash better than anyone has ever done it.

Some of you will think that this will backfire but if you are willing to "take out the trash" without complaining and set new standards for some menial task, you will not be doing that task for long.

Leaders will see your enthusiasm and dream of how hard you will work on a more meaningful task if you can commit such energy to "taking out the trash." I have "taken out the trash"

many times in my career and I still do it regularly: never think that you are too good to "take out the trash."

A friend of mine, Bob Kehoe, an internet entrepreneur, provided another vivid statement to capture this aspect of becoming indispensable: "grab the heaviest thing!" captures the blue collar aspect of the attitude needed to have career success.

When complaining about having to work late on a proposal – grab the heaviest thing! When your office is downsizing because of a contract being eliminated – grab the heaviest thing! When your 8-to-5 job is painfully easy – grab the heaviest thing!

Exude passion, energy, and balance. Let's get started!

II. MAKE YOUR OWN LUCK

Stop wondering why your neighbor got a new job or why your cousin has been happy at his current job for 20 years. Stop talking about how lucky they are and start making your own luck. The three dimensions of being indispensable are (1) strengthening your core, (2) refining how you interact with others, and (3) investing in your future. The three dimensions are equally important, mutually supporting, and incrementally applied. I will detail them from inside out: strong core, then interaction with others, and, last, investing in the future.

Dimensions of Career Success

Just like your body, without a strong core you are not healthy and you cannot do other more complex and challenging exercises or activities. Many of these core features are used in the other two dimensions. Instead of calculating, you will think; you will consider context when applying tools. Instead of merely spewing facts, you will communicate with compelling parables. You will go beyond complying to creating something of value that remains when you complete a project.

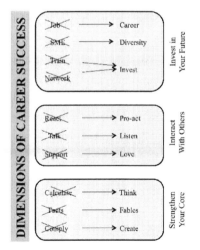

Make Yourself Indispensable

The second dimension of career success focuses on how you interact with others. Most important, treat everyone the same: do not coddle your boss and then treat a subordinate with disrespect. Treat everyone with honesty and dignity. Be patient but with a purpose. Understand the importance of listening over talking. A leader is not one who commands respect but one who earns it.

To become indispensable, you must go beyond supporting efforts, you have to love them. Passion is underrated – if you do not feel strongly that your job is important and that you can be fantastic at doing it then you probably will not be great. Maya Angelou said it best...

> "I've learned that people will forget what you said, people will forget what you did, but people will never forget how you made them feel."

Interact with people with that in mind!

The last dimension to be covered, investing in your future, is where you take a strategic view of your career, lay out the map, and point to your destination. A major factor of a successful career is the recognition of the difference between "what" and "how." Being a subject matter expert (SME) is wonderful as long as you excel in appreciating context and process in addition to mastering the content. Embracing cognitive diversity within yourself and the people you work with is critical. Last, you will learn to treat your dealings with your career, such as training and networking, as investments. Your career is like a retirement plan: save early and often; let compound interest work for you!

26

Make Yourself Indispensable

A. STRENGTHEN YOUR CORE

Be the Great Communicator

Quality communication is the key component of building a strong core that empowers career success and, thus, helps you to be seen as indispensable. The first impulse is to assume that communication is about providing inspiring speeches and motivational talks. While these are valuable, being a quality communicator requires skills in both transmitting and receiving information.

My favorite rule is to listen, learn, and write things down. Without a desire and skill to listen, when you finally do start to talk or write, you will not have sufficient content (relevant knowledge) or context (appropriate perspective) to provide a meaningful message.

> "Listen, learn, and write things down."

Communication is an important factor all throughout the innovation process for both team building and development of a specific solution. In a recent Harvard Business Review article, David McCullough stated that if he were asked to create a curriculum for a business school leadership program he would focus on the criticality of listening. He would emphasize the art of asking good questions and recognizing what people *do not* say. (McCollough, 2008)

27

Make Yourself Indispensable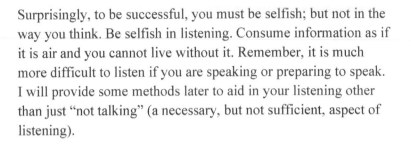

Surprisingly, to be successful, you must be selfish; but not in the way you think. Be selfish in listening. Consume information as if it is air and you cannot live without it. Remember, it is much more difficult to listen if you are speaking or preparing to speak. I will provide some methods later to aid in your listening other than just "not talking" (a necessary, but not sufficient, aspect of listening).

Most brilliant people can describe their insights and technical breakthroughs compellingly. However, productive people also have the skill and inclination to see the value in listening to others in order to advance their own concepts further, make others feel good about themselves, and contribute positively to team dynamics. These behaviors will refine your innovation skills and make you a valuable part of any team, maybe even indispensable.

Any message is transmitted in two parts: content and context. The content (the actual words) represents only 10% of the message. The context contains 90% of the meaning of the message.

The context is equally split between tone of voice and body language. Tone of voice includes volume, rate, clarity, and mood. Body language includes posture, openness of stance, standing vs sitting, synchronicity of movement with content, and facial expression.

Type of Messaging	Dimensions with Percent Contribution to Message		
	Content (10%)	Tone of Voice (45%)	Body Language (45%)
Text/E-Mail	X		
Telephone Conversation	X	X	
Face-to-Face	X	X	X

Clearly, "listening" does not just happen with one's ears; it also includes watching and "feeling" the person talking.

> "The context contains 90% of the meaning of the message; content provides only 10%."

James Heskett of the Harvard Business School suggests that using "the gentle art of asking instead of telling" has been lost. (Heskett, 2014) He even believes that we have stopped listening, even to ourselves, so we are definitely not attuned to what others are saying to us.

Why might we have forgotten how to listen? I think that it is because it requires concentration and patience – two things in short supply with most people's hypersensitivity to "immediate information gratification[3]."

Two approaches to improving listening skills are by empathy and by writing.

---

[3] This is a term I coined for the huddled masses yearning to Google their way through life...

Make Yourself Indispensable

Listen by Empathy

A key roadblock to good communication is a person's tendency to judge. Fortunately, if you can learn to listen with the goal to understand, you can minimize your evaluative impulses and greatly improve your communication with others. (Rogers, 1991)

Genuine listening means suspending memory, desire, and judgment – and, for a few moments at least, existing for the other person. When listening is genuine, the emphasis is on the speaker, not the listener." (Nichols, 1995)

> "Genuine listening means suspending memory, desire, and judgment – and, for a few moments at least, existing for the other person. When listening is genuine, the emphasis is on the speaker, not the listener."   (Nichols, 1995)

While "active" listening sounds contradictory, the ability to focus on other peoples' needs and wants (over your own) and incorporate them into a shared understanding of a problem does take energy and finesse.

Most people decide whether they will listen within the first 15 seconds of a conversation, so as the receiver of information you must establish that you are going to listen and not just talk (or prepare to talk). Without this conscious effort, you will likely tune people out and miss out on potentially useful information.

Good communication goes both ways (transmit and receive) but work on receiving because transmitting comes naturally to most everyone.[4]

Make Yourself Indispensable

Why is active listening not used more widely? (Nichols, 1995) First, it stems from a lack of courage to walk in someone else's shoes. Second, heightened emotions inhibit listening. Real opportunities for a collective breakthrough are usually related to topics where heated discussions have already happened. In these cases, it may be useful to employ a moderator (third party). Last, the larger the group the more difficult it is to focus on the message and remain focused through interruptions.

On a related note, how do you measure the success of an interview (assume that *you* are being interviewed)? In a successful interview, you want the interviewer(s) to talk more than you. If you can make this happen, they will inevitably have a greater satisfaction with the interview and, in turn, with you. Why is that the case?

Haven't you joked about how "people love to hear themselves talk"? It is true, so when you are listening you are actually building the esteem of the presenter and his or her impression of the interaction with you.

In addition, for an interview the more interviewers talk, the more they share about the position under consideration, the organization, and what makes a successful new hire. You can often get significant information in an interview just by listening! There will be much more on this topic later in the book when Roger discusses "winning" the interview.

---

[4] Similarly, when I coached youth soccer, I always focused more on defense since offense (i.e., scoring goals) came naturally to most of the players.

Make Yourself Indispensable

Listen by Writing

How do you really *listen* to other people; let the words sink in so you may digest them? If you are tempted to ask a question or interrupt, jot down a note so you do not forget the point about which you are curious. This intellectual restraint is a great technique that supports active listening.

If you write down a question (rather than asking it when it pops into your head) you may find that the speaker answers it before you have a chance to ask. So, be patient!

In addition, writing down a question or just some highlight you find useful is an act that helps to engender trust between you and the speaker.

I have noticed that even the act of bringing a notebook and pen to place in front of you provides encouragement to the speaker and prompts your brain to listen.

Facial and body language cues have been found to be quite important for communication. For instance, if you smile enough your mood will brighten and if you stand tall in an open stance you will be more confident. (Hanna, 2010)

Therefore, if you make a habit of using a pen and pad of paper as an indicator that you are entering a listening mode, your body and brain will respond. A benefit of this approach is having notes of an interaction that might be useful in their own right, especially to help you master the information provided to you. This is especially true during a job interview.

Make Yourself Indispensable

> "Just the act of bringing a notebook and pen to place in front of you for a meeting or presentation provides encouragement to the speaker and prompts your brain to listen."

Once you have heard a message, you can ask questions for clarification, not to impress people or belittle the speaker. A real listener does not ask a question that starts with "I was thinking…" but rather say "you mentioned earlier… could you comment on how you…" The questions should be about understanding the speaker better rather than trying to show people that you know more than the speaker.

Interestingly, I have found that if you disagree with someone's conclusion it is likely that one will start to argue about the conclusion. However, normally the reason for a disagreement is something that was *not* stated rather than something that *was* stated. It is usually something as simple as unstated assumptions or differences in the use of the same terminology.

> "Normally the reason for a disagreement is something that was *not* stated rather than something that *was* stated."

Even when I was a student at the U.S. Air Force Academy, I had already started my application of my favorite saying: "listen, learn, and write things down."

Make Yourself Indispensable

I was well-known for my near-microfiche index cards on which I would cram all of the salient facts for an upcoming test for courses such as Thermodynamics, Philosophy, or Law for Military Officers. I did this so I would have the material ready to study when I had a few spare minutes in study hall or standing in formation (remember, this was a military academy). I even used to pull them out before the lights went down at the movie theater while on dates. Sadly, this is not an exaggeration, as my wife of thirty-three years can attest.

What I discovered from writing these study cards was that the process of organizing and writing down the material helped me learn the material much better. As a result, it is always "listen" first, but you pick what comes second and third (write then learn *or* learn then write).

As Michael Gelb said, "great thinkers listen first."

"Great thinkers listen first."   Michael Gelb

In summary, a key obstacle to good communication is the tendency to evaluate. (Rogers, 1991) Fortunately, if people can improve their listening skills, they can reduce their inclination to judge and greatly improve their communications with others. You can even train yourself with a pen and pad of paper to disrupt the urge to interrupt the speaker.

Be selfish… Listen!

Time to Transmit

Make Yourself Indispensable

Of course, at some point you must engage in a dialogue but having followed these listening tips you hopefully will have delayed your impulse to interrupt or pass judgment. You might even have found yourself learning something new and when you finally ask a question or provide a comment, it will be more composed and thoughtful.

In creating that compelling message at your job, in a final report, in a team meeting, etc. it is critical to focus on parables over facts. Facts are passive, tedious, and forgettable while parables are active, interesting, and memorable. Facts are content; parables are content plus context.

Our minds are finite but it seems that we have so much information to either absorb or transmit; how can we do it? Cognitive psychologists say that we can be helped by chunking or grouping information into logical sequences so that we remember more.

Can you remember a sequence of ten random numbers easily? Well, we often do when we learn a telephone number with an area code followed by three digits and then finally the four digit extension. Try to remember ten numbers without grouping them in some way; it is much more difficult.

I say to focus on parables over facts. A parable or story is an interesting way to present multiple facts in a memorable way. Do not provide 30 beautiful beads and expect your audience to imagine the necklace it would make. You must give them the thread (i.e., storyline) onto which you hang the beads (i.e., facts).

In this way, the parable becomes the assemblage of the facts which is much easier to recall than the individual facts.

"Focus on parables over facts."

A few of my favorite parables are not only good examples to review for context but they actually have relevant content to describe how to empower quality communication. Several short vignettes follow to provide some examples of "parables over facts."

"Bridge Extrema": To provide a memorable message, your words must stand out from the onslaught of information coming at people. One way to do this is to pair words that are normally not associated as a way to make them more compelling (and memorable). Being a "pragmatic visionary" sounds like an interesting thing to be: forward-thinking yet practical.

"Bridge extrema to reach your audience."

Another "bridge extrema" combination is to describe the business of making glue, razors, straws, etc. as "fascinatingly mundane." Commodity items that are fairly basic are compelling because we cannot live without them and there is a very resilient demand for years (if not forever). Think about it, what if you made one cent on every straw ever produced? Straws are fascinatingly mundane!

In the 2000 U.S. Presidential Campaign, George W. Bush called himself a "passionate conservative," two terms not often used in the same breath. He not only caught peoples' attention, he won the election.

"Use Verbs, Not Adjectives": In any approach used to inspire individual and organizational performance, one must use "people verbs" (i.e., actions that people take, not activities that occur in organizations).

For example, when asked to "align their efforts with strategic objectives" it is difficult to expect that people will know what behavior will satisfy this policy. However, if they are told to "listen, learn, and write things down when attending interdepartmental meetings," they have clear actionable behaviors to model.

If you say that "performance is job one" your employees will have no idea what to do. Yet, challenging them to "complete every deliverable one week early" (to permit an extra round of enhancements) makes the value proposition for expected actions clear. More importantly, it links the actions to the desired results (i.e., makes them traceable).

> "Use people verbs, not adjectives."

Adjectives are normally value judgments rather than statements of facts, so avoid them unless they are based on verbs. For example, "the compelling story" is more impactful than "the extraordinary plot."

It is important to remember (a la Maya Angelou) that people usually do not remember what you say but they do remember the emotion you elicit: excitement, awe, love, etc. Use this to your advantage by trying to focus on action over adjectives.

"Draw a Picture to Build a Team": The very act of a team contributing to a figure collectively provides opportunities to refine terminology, share problem solving skills, appreciate alternative approaches, and integrate team inputs effectively.

This technique will likely yield results more quickly than reviewing text or going on-line! It is a great technique to enhance team dynamics by having members work together (face-to-face) on a diagram representing the problem being addressed or the solution being proposed. This is better than using an on-line collaboration tool which can be impersonal and will likely elicit or proliferate misunderstandings between team members.

"Draw a picture to build a team."

While the product of a picture-drawing process may be valuable, the relationships established amongst the team members will provide value in the form of enduring respect and understanding. In this case, the process may be more valuable than the product.

In summary, listening with positive intent and speaking/writing with clarity will provide a good start at you becoming a polished communicator. To be seen as indispensable, you must continually refine your communication skills. Next, we will examine our career habits and work ethic as part of our core capabilities.

Focus, Fight, and Feedback

Make Yourself Indispensable

Success is not about talent, it is about hard work and creating opportunity. A classic book on success metrics clearly characterizes "hard work" as thousands of hours of deliberate practice focused on improving performance. (Gladwell, 2008)

For example, *expert* violinists will have logged more than 10,000 hours of practice by the time they are twenty years old. Conversely, people aiming to be a music teacher had practiced only 4,000 hours total by the time they turned twenty years old.

Unfortunately, for many people their circumstances do not permit them to be able to commit 1,000 hours a year (about 2 hours and 45 minutes a day, every day of the year). Mozart (piano), Tiger Woods (golf), David Beckham (soccer), and the Williams sisters (tennis) had all logged over 10,000 hours of focused practice by the time they were in their mid-teens; they were not child prodigies! They were lucky they had the family situation where they could allocate so much time on focused practice at such a young age (i.e., opportunity) but there was no genetic luck involved.

There is no evidence that genetics has much of anything to do with real success. Persistence at a high level of intensity (nominally 1,000 hours a year for ten years) is the only repeatable, reliable metric for success. This is not just true for musicians but for every field studied: sports, science, poetry, etc. It was found that most took ten years from starting their profession until they did their best work. (Syed, 2010)

Make Yourself Indispensable

> "Do you want to be at the top of your field? Just spend about 2 hours and 45 minutes per day for ten years focusing on skills critical for your success."

The retired race car driver Bobby Unser, noted that "Desire! That's the one secret of every man's career. Not education. Not being born with hidden talents." You must begin now to understand what you want to be in life and develop the skills to the level of proficiency that assures success. Work hard!

There is always a place in an organization for someone willing to work hard and go beyond what is expected of them. (Huckabee, 2012) Mike Huckabee has applied both political savvy and literary wit to his many books. I summarize in the table below some of his practical job-specific advice from his writings into "Huckabee's Highlights."

Huckabee's Highlights	
Job	Actions
- No one owes you a job, it is a privilege.	- Get in early and stay late. There is no substitute for energy.
- If you accept a job, you owe them.	- Do your work without being asked once or twice.
- A job is never perfect.	- Do the worst tasks first.
	- Be humble.

Your core mission must be to apply meaning to your endeavors weekly, daily, hourly; fight to have the discipline to put the extra time in on basics to build the foundation for excellence. This

Make Yourself Indispensable

includes being open to critique, especially from those you pattern your career after; a key aspect of purposeful practice is feedback.

What attribute must you hone to satisfy your career's ambition? Start today focusing some time on activities to support this development.

Early in my career, I focused on writing things down. I now publish a monthly essay on innovation and workforce productivity to continually sharpen my writing and analytic abilities. I have made these efforts part of my "day" job so my 2 hours and 45 minutes of deliberate practice daily is part of my regular work day.

Individuals who believe that hard work is more important than talent actually work harder and do indeed perform better and are recognized for it. This also works in the classroom. If students are praised for their intelligence (reinforcing the talent myth) their success is much more fleeting than those who are praised for their hard work.

The students who are praised for their efforts not only performed better but they were more likely to attempt more difficult future tasks. Conversely, people who are continually told they are "intelligent" are afraid to have their intelligence banner torn down so they are actually more apprehensive about trying more difficult tasks.

Another problem with encouraging the talent myth is that if you are not successful quickly, you feel betrayed by the world. It takes time for you to hone your skills and the thought that talent is more important than hard work makes people either lazy or focused on the wrong priorities. So, if you want to encourage better performance, praise effort not talent.

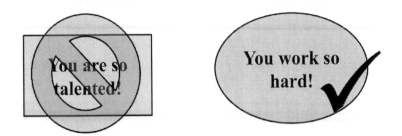

Sports have a built-in feedback mechanism: if you lose, you probably need to make some changes. However, if you win you must be doing something right.[5] This may be broken down into very small units since you cannot always win but you can concentrate on pitching more strikeouts in baseball, improving your free throw percentage in basketball, etc.

Breaking down a larger goal into components and attacking each small one in succession (being incrementally aggressive) increases your chances of success.

---

[5] Please note, for youth and amateur sports, winning should not be the ultimate goal but since for most sports we do keep score, it is likely that most people will acknowledge and consider victories and losses.

Make Yourself Indispensable

> "Breaking down a larger goal into components and attacking each small one in succession (i.e., be incrementally aggressive) increases your chances of success."

For business, this might be more difficult because success is seldom an individual activity; organizational success generally results from teamwork. Still, you might be able to get a sense of your improvement by monitoring intermediate achievements such as writing a research paper to be published in a refereed journal, a customer making a by-name request for your services, or improving your proposal win rate over time. These are all potential business or professional metrics you can scrutinize.

In addition, sports are more zero-sum games because if you win the racquetball match, by definition, your opponent loses. However, in business, you and your colleagues can all benefit from your performance which shockingly often leads some people to work less. It is sad, but true, that without having clear winners or losers, some business people will not work as hard.

Applying this concept to the corporate environment or decision making situations suggests that a critical aspect of any decision framework is how the data is linked. This is the context or metadata (i.e., data about data) which shows relevant organizational insights and relationships. Decision models have been sold in the past as panaceas that only require subject matter experts in a specified area to create quality outcomes. However, you need a subject matter expert who appreciates and understands the importance of how the content is aggregated into

Make Yourself Indispensable

a body of knowledge and applied under changing conditions
(i.e., the context).

Experts are able to fight the inevitable runaway of data of any
domain by filtering out extraneous information and focusing on
the most critical facts. An expert tennis player can "read" the
hips and shoulders of an opponent serving to know exactly
where the serve is going to go. Similarly, an expert in a scientific
domain can filter out irrelevant data that might lead a novice to
an incorrect conclusion or chew up a lot of resources
determining the utility of some outlying data.

In this way, good decision making is the ability to reduce content
into patterns. I worked for a man named Bob LaRose who was
very successful at business and he said the simple secret to
business was recognizing patterns and acting accordingly. The
ability to do this comes from – you guessed it – deliberate
practice.

> "The secret to business is recognizing patterns
> and acting accordingly."   Bob LaRose

If you go through your business life reacting to situations and
taking every day as a new day, no amount of business experience
will lead to success. However, if you concentrate on observing
how things affect each other, what techniques are successful,
under what conditions performance is maximized, and you *write
it down*, you will get better at making quality decisions.

In summary, purposeful practice is an important feature of having a strong foundation for success. You must define your goal clearly and then act accordingly. Practice does not make perfect; it makes permanent. Therefore, you need to have the help of a coach or mentor to truly be successful.

As you pursue success in your career, positive outcomes result from focusing on the basics so that as a situation becomes complex you see the relevant thread through the fog of the irrelevant and "pull it" to your full advantage.

The Science of Thinking

The brain is not a simple organ and its importance to our ability to perform at the highest levels on everything from sports and music to decision making and problem solving is profound.

Generally speaking, there are three activities that can empower better thinking: physical exercise, deliberate learning, and focused meditation. A common theme in all three activities is again "how you do it is more important than what you do."

> "There are three activities that can empower better thinking: physical exercise, deliberate learning, and focused meditation."

Three performance factors apply to each activity: intensity, frequency, and duration. Of these three, intensity is the most important. It represents the effort or focus one puts into the task coupled with the process of having challenging, yet achievable,

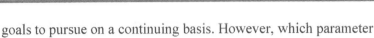
goals to pursue on a continuing basis. However, which parameter is next most important depends on your eventual objective.

For everyday goals, frequency is next most important factor. However, to attain world class performance, duration is the next most important dimension. For regular people, just trying to stay healthy, having a single weekly 3-hour physical workout, meditation sequence, or study session is not as good as six separate intense 30-minute efforts spread throughout the week.

PRIORITIES IN PERFORMANCE

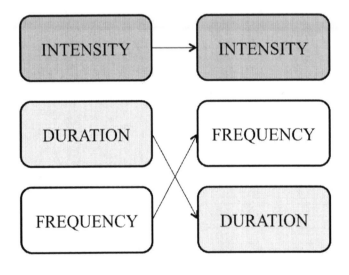

For superstars and olympians…

For the rest of us

Make Yourself Indispensable

Intense activities that last only 10-30 minutes can provide tangible results. In addition, once you make daily activities in these three dimensions (exercising, learning, and meditation) a habit, it is much easier to maintain and improve performance. (Cornell, 1996)

I work out every weekday morning. It is as natural as grabbing the morning paper or brushing my teeth after a meal. As you make it the norm to exercise, learn, and meditate daily, you will need to mix up your exact efforts periodically to avoid boredom.

For example, for years I used a daily form of meditation at bedtime called focusing but recently I went back to a breathing-based technique that I also do during the day. I also switch up my physical workout structure periodically to stay motivated and avoid overuse injuries.

I have already discussed the importance of duration for attaining a world class level of performance. In reality, to attain expert levels one must act with high intensity, long duration, *and* high frequency (at least daily). How else can one get to 10,000 hours of deliberate practice over ten years. Remember that if you want to be a world-class accountant, engineer, nurse, etc.

Exercising, Learning, and Meditation

Physical fitness and cognitive fitness are intimately related. Being in good physical shape helps the functioning of the brain which in turn enhances your cognitive abilities. It improves your ability to perform cognitively by providing the most efficient brain possible. Studies have shown that exercise helps lower

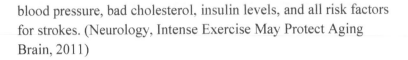
blood pressure, bad cholesterol, insulin levels, and all risk factors for strokes. (Neurology, Intense Exercise May Protect Aging Brain, 2011)

> "The best way to a healthy mind is through a healthy body."

Studies showed that exercising one hour, three times a week, for three months produced increased cerebral flow, enhanced memory, and increased neurogenesis (i.e., making new baby neurons that link disparate information). (Strauch, 2005) My personal experience supports this assertion, because I feel lethargic and dull-witted when I do not work out regularly.

Simple aerobic exercise performed regularly improves episodic memory and organizational functions by about 20 percent, finds Art Kramer of the University of Illinois at Urbana-Champaign. His studies have mostly been done on older adults, so it's possible the results apply only to people whose brain physiology has begun to deteriorate which, unfortunately, may happen as early as our 20s. Exercise aids in the creation of new neurons in the region of the hippocampus, which stores experiences and new knowledge.

> "Exercise aids in the creation of new neurons which enables storing new knowledge."

Muscle contraction stimulates the production of neuron fertilizers such as brain-derived neurotrophic factor (BDNF) and neurotransmitters (that carry brain signals). Normally, growth-factor molecules (such as BDNF) are too large to make it through the blood-brain barrier but for reasons that are still unknown, exercise makes that barrier more porous, allowing those growth enablers to get through and help stimulate neuron growth.

Exercise also stimulates the production of new synapses, the connections that constitute functional circuits and whose capacity and efficiency underlie superior intelligence.

Similarly, taking up a new, cognitively demanding activity such as ballroom dancing or learning a foreign language is likely to boost processing speed and improve memory. You must challenge yourself to improve; limited discomfort from intense effort *is* a reasonable objective (though it is not absolutely necessary) for both physical and cognitive benefits. As I said before, making yourself indispensable requires diligence.

People who exercise with greater intensity are significantly less likely to show brain damage caused by blocked arteries than people who exercise lightly. There is actually no difference between those who exercised lightly and those who did not exercise at all. Remember, intensity is the most important factor for any physical or intellectual activity.

> "Intensity is the most important factor for any physical or intellectual activity."

My advice to you is to establish a habit of moderate to strenuous exercise 4-5 days a week and improvements to your cognitive fitness will parallel your enhanced physical fitness. It does not have to be running but it must be a deliberate aerobic challenge performed regularly. I know, I know, there are many brilliant, creative couch potatoes. The hypothesis is that they could be even better if they ran around the park rather than to the cookie jar.

> "Establish a habit of moderate to strenuous exercise 4-5 days a week and improvements to your cognitive fitness will parallel your enhanced physical fitness."

Evidence suggests that deliberate mental challenges can contribute to keeping the brain functioning optimally but we must stay engaged and active with intellectually-diverse activities. New neurons are produced when we focus on a task that is highly complex but we also know that only half of new brain cells survive; therefore, you are always fighting an uphill physical and cognitive battle, especially after the age of twenty or thirty. As a result, you really need to be making a lot of new brain cells to have a significant net growth because some of the old, existing ones are also dying off. Intellectually-stimulating games, such as crossword puzzles, also provide a simple means to keep learning through deliberate, challenging cognitive work.

> "Intellectually-stimulating games provide a simple means to continually keep learning and promote brain performance."

Make Yourself Indispensable

A study of air traffic controllers showed that in abilities such as processing speed, younger air traffic controllers did better in cognitive tests. Yet, in two important cognitive functions – visual orientation *(the capacity to look at a plane in two dimensions on a computer screen and imagine it in three dimensions in the sky)* and dealing with ambiguity *(coping well with conflicting information, computer crashes, or even the possibility that the computer might be wrong)* – older air traffic controllers did just as well.

These observations apply equally to other professions. Therefore, more experienced brains may not be able to memorize as well but they may discern patterns more quickly and accurately which will contribute to success. So, when it comes to thinking, the old adage of "you are not getting older, you are getting better" may indeed be true.

In order to enhance brain function it is important to not just *use* your brain; you must *challenge* it by providing ever increasing stimulation in either depth (difficulty) or breadth (variety). Try to learn something new daily. Continual learning is a trait of almost all successful (and indispensable) people.

> "Continual learning is a trait of almost all successful (and indispensable) people."

There is significant commonality between how you continue to improve physically versus cognitively. We stated earlier the importance of deliberate practice with regular and challenging activity. If you can do ten push-ups, is doing five push-ups a tough workout? No. You try to do as many as possible in the first set and then do your best in the second set, even if it means only doing six in the second set. You must challenge yourself!

You should do the same thing cognitively. If you do crossword puzzles that you can complete easily in fifteen minutes then crossword puzzles probably will not enhance your cognitive fitness if you continue to do puzzles with the same level of difficulty. However, if you concentrate on continually trying more challenging crossword puzzles or trying to do them faster or even applying different solution techniques, you will gain cognitive benefits.

Get out of your comfort zone! As I told my physics students years ago, you learn the most after a slight period of confusion. What was true in my physics classroom over 25 years ago is still true today.

> "You learn the most after a slight period of confusion."

Physical exercise demonstrably *increases* the rate of neurogenesis and mental exercise helps *ensure the survival* of any newly created neurons. Today, these activities usually take place in very different venues: the former, in health clubs; the latter, in academic settings. It appears that the borders between physical and mental exercise will become less pronounced in the future.

Make Yourself Indispensable

Expect new programs such as brain fitness podcasts that will allow us to train working memory as we jog or use stationary bikes with built-in brain games. (Top 10 Brain Training Future Trends, 2012) These combination routines provide opportunities for especially efficient activities just as one might do physical exercises that target the arms and abs simultaneously.

The contents of memory provide the very foundation of the analytic process. Whatever affects how well that information is recalled from memory will also affect the quality of the decision making process. As a result, information really provides the building blocks for innovation, productivity, and enhanced decision making.

> "Information serves as the building blocks for innovation, productivity, and decision making."

Foundational research by George Miller from the 1950s showed that no more than seven simple items (such as varying musical notes or subtle differences in volume) can be recalled reliably. (Miller, 1956) While Miller pushes hard *not* to assume that seven is some magical number, he does note that it appears often in literature, everyday life, and history: seven seas, seven deadly sins, seven wonders of the world, seven levels of hell, seven primary colors, seven notes of the musical scale, seven digits in a phone number, seven days of the week, etc. Possibly, the fact that humans have this innate physiological limitation is a constraint that has led to these many lists of seven.

Make Yourself Indispensable

While Miller's work shows that seven is a number for humans to be able to maximally discriminate, we have found over the years that in most situations humans do not perform optimally. In reality, people are very good at remembering and applying lists of items or dimensions of problems that are between three and five.

Our hypothesis is supported by research that states four items—not seven—is the more likely cognitive threshold for working memory. (Moskowitz, 27 April 2008) Seven is achieved only if examining very simple characteristics or if the people are well-rested and motivated!

> "People learn facts better in clumps of no larger than three to five."

How do we actually consume tidbits of useful information in the brain to learn? A useful axiom I told my physics students was that people typically learn 10% of what they read; 20% of what they hear; 30% of what they see in visuals; and 90% of what they "do" (in real life or in a simulation). (Penenberg, 2011) Each successive mode is a more focused and effective activity for the learner: read → hear → see → speak →do.

Another means of cognitive enhancement (in addition to deliberate learning and exercise) is meditation. Meditation is not just lying around and doing nothing; it requires deliberate activities to encourage your mind to focus on alternative issues from your day-to-day grind. Being lazy is not being spiritual!

Make Yourself Indispensable

"Being lazy is not being spiritual!"

Meditation can strengthen regions of the brain that control attention and process sensory signals from the outside world. In a program that neuroscientist Amishi Jha of the University of Miami calls mindfulness-based mind-fitness training, participants build concentration by focusing on one object, such as a particular body sensation. The training, she says, has shown success in enhancing mental agility and attention "by changing brain structure and function so that brain processes are more efficient," a capability often associated with higher intelligence. (Begley, 2011)

A constructive mood also promotes creative problem solving. In this case, reducing stress permits underlying skills to reach their full potential.

Finally, being told that you belong to a group that does well on a test tends to help you do better than if you're told you belong to a group that does poorly. The latter floods you with cortisol, while the former gives you the inspiration, via a dopamine surge, to keep plugging away. (Begley, 2011) This complex cause and effect sequence is what I consider the self-fulfilling prophecy: if you think you will do well, it is more likely that you will do well. Having a positive attitude is a critical component for becoming indispensable both for your own mental processes and the impression you make on others.

Chronic stress and anxiety, no matter whether induced by external events or by your own thoughts, are the opposite of exercise: they prevent the creation of new neurons and inhibit clear thinking. (Fernandez, 2007) However, I have found that stress normally does not come from hard work but, rather, from lack of control.

> "Stress does not come from hard work, it comes from lack of control."

The benefits of meditation span physiology, psychology, and spirituality; the top five specific tailored contributions from meditation are detailed below. (Frederik, 2013)

1. Increases exercise tolerance – permits you to perform more physical exercise (which has already been shown to aid cognitive fitness);
2. Improves learning ability and memory – improves direct cognitive performance;
3. Increases listening skills and empathy – directly improves learning and teamwork;
4. Helps with focus and concentration – permits you to perform with greater intensity; and
5. Creates greater orderliness of brain functioning – a force multiplier across all cognitive activities.

The Dalai Lama XIV stated that "sleep is the best meditation." (Sleep is the Best Meditation, 2010) While this interpretation is debatable, sleep as an enabler to cognitive health cannot be refuted. Studies have shown even deliberate training is not sufficient to create short-term and long-term memory stores, whereas a good night's sleep is necessary. (Donlea, 24 June 2011)

In summary, the science of thinking shows clearly that physical exercise, deliberate learning, and focused meditation separately and together enhance cognitive fitness.

This improved brain health contributes to higher productivity and likelihood of innovation by individuals. Since organizations do not perform, people do; an organization full of thinking individuals will produce greater organizational performance. This is a critical component of a strong core needed to power your career along a path toward success.

> "Organizations do not perform. People do!"

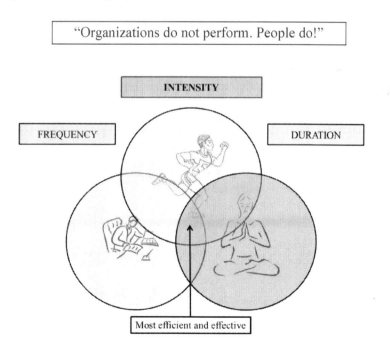

Most efficient and effective

Make Yourself Indispensable

Beware of Pandora's Internet

The internet not only delivers good and bad information more quickly than ever before, the process by which it is delivered actually changes us. The interrupt-driven technologies are teaching us *not* to think, just browse. Unfortunately, unlike when books *offset and augmented* the oratory tradition, the internet is *replacing* reading for many people. Some feel that the benefit of getting so much information so quickly makes up for the lack of understanding and synthesis. I do not agree.

Synthesis is the key act that is lacking in individuals who frequent the internet, yet synthesis is also a necessary skill of an indispensable person. The information is presented on the internet but there is no encouragement or requirement to assess what all of these facts mean together. There is not the time, nor the need, to ponder what the information all means in aggregate.

The context is always critical to understanding what information means but context on the internet is being replaced by more and more content.

My mantra of focusing on parables over facts is more important now than ever for internet usage. As all of the information flows, trying to document the information into a series of unifying parables or overarching principles, will help to prevent some of the deleterious effects of the internet. For this to be truly effective, one must take time (with the computer off) to think how the streams of data are related.

Make Yourself Indispensable

> "One must take time (with the computer off) to think how streams of data are related."

The use of hypertext provides the context for how information is related; however, to investigate the sidebar it often takes the user further and further from the core document. How many times have you clicked on a hypertext link, then on another, and before you knew it, you could not remember the document you started reading in the first place?

An experiment demonstrated that readers who consumed information linearly (i.e., reading straight through a text document) scored better on comprehension tests than those who consumed it through hypertext links. (Carr, 2011) It is theorized that the hypertext-using reader did not truly synthesize the information as fully as those who read all of the material without the distraction of moving to another page.

For all of these reasons, I suggest that you actually read books to keep your cognitive fitness at its peak to support your pursuit of career success.

> "Read books to keep your cognitive fitness at its peak to support your pursuit of career success."

If you use only the internet for consuming new information your brain gets used to rapid-fire, shallow exchanges of content. Researchers have even described their thinking and writing taking on a "staccato" style with a choppy, erratic pace as the result of using the internet.[6] (Carr, 2011)

Make Yourself Indispensable

It is not just actions that can alter brain operations. Even thinking about the rapid fire accessing of data will cause the brain to continue to reinforce neural paths for this type of activity. We are how we think!

One of the computers' greatest strengths, from a productivity perspective, is also its greatest detriment to deep cognitive thought: focusing on interruptions. Alerts remind us of meetings, grocery list items, and picking up a child at school and permit us to focus our intellectual energies to other domains knowing that the computer will reliably and accurately warn us of oncoming events that need attention.

However, the computer also informs us of many, many things that are going on that are irrelevant or simply distracting. Twitter feeds that tell you when your favorite actor or actress is sitting down to eat or Facebook posts of friends heading out of town to see relatives create distractions that impose switching costs on your brain.

Every time you switch your brain's attention to information that is not relevant to your current activity, it costs you in effectiveness and time. Even being informed of incoming e-mails or receiving web site alerts, such as when new information needed for your work or studies come in, still distracts from your train of thought.

---

[6] This account sounds very similar to Nietzche's comment about using a typewriter rather than ink and quill decades ago.

Make Yourself Indispensable

> "Every time you switch your brain's attention to information that is not relevant to your current activity, it costs you in effectiveness and time."

The key is to be able to turn off the distractions when you need to think deeply. You *can* still think deeply while on the computer or on the internet; you just need to focus for a period of time on one thing and let it really sink in and connect with existing information. Do not expect or allow the computer or the internet to do that for you. Once you give up the job of synthesis and thinking to the computer, it will be difficult to get it back.

A mantra that I use to accentuate this principle is "turn it off to turn it on." Turn off the interrupt-driven electronic devices and applications to turn on your productivity. The brain will perform optimally if you focus on a given activity deeply and exclusively for 90 minutes at a time. Less than this, you may not make a sufficient impression of the material for it to be retained.

> "Turn it off to turn it on."

If you try to work longer than this you will start to lose your focus and be less effective. By scripting these 90-minute cognitive bursts, you can manage the tendency of the internet (or any distraction) to prevent you from learning and executing optimally.

The use of the internet is valuable for the available content and even in some of the skills that you can learn such as eye-hand coordination, skimming for key facts, and searching for potential

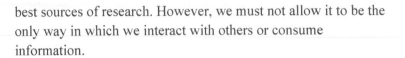

best sources of research. However, we must not allow it to be the only way in which we interact with others or consume information.

In 2009, Patricia Greenfield hypothesized that "every medium develops some cognitive skills at the expense of others." For the internet, she suggests that our visual-spatial intelligence has been enhanced while the deep thinking needed for improved knowledge retention, logical reasoning, and introspection have waned. This has been evidenced by the continual rise in Intelligence Quotient (IQ) scores on enhanced visual and contextual processing despite a reduction in ability in vocabulary, general knowledge acquisition, and arithmetic. (Greenfield, January 2009)

Get Your Brain in Shape[7]

There are ways to fight this potential neural atrophy. Any set of activities that is engaging (*i.e., interesting, often via a reward system*), novel (*change the type of activities*), and adaptive (*continually make the activities challenging*) will assist you in improving brain performance.

Reading is one such activity. Research has reinforced what many of us believe without proof: reading helps your brain. While for many, reading provides enjoyment and relaxation short-term; long-term it has been shown to create cognitive reserve that protects the brain from aging effects.

---

[7]Adapted from Lumosity, http://www.lumosity.com/the-science/key-concepts, 2011.

Make Yourself Indispensable

However, it is emphasized that benefits are accrued for those who avidly read a wide variety of challenging content. Reading the comics and restaurant menus does not suffice!

The foundational ways of measuring cognitive performance are processing speed (*rate of logical operations*) and neuroplasticity (*the brain's ability to adapt to new challenges by rewiring itself*). These are foundational because higher level capabilities depend on them and they are also the most difficult to enhance.

Working memory is the ability to store, access, use, and move content into and out of long-term memory and from your environment.

Improvements to working memory enhance both short-term and long-term brain performance. Short-term brain performance is

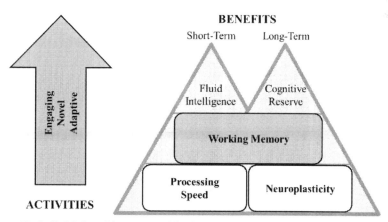

called fluid intelligence. This is the ability to sort, filter, and

Make Yourself Indispensable

assemble information into logical frameworks to support quality decision making and predictive capabilities.

Cognitive reserve is the long-term resiliency of the brain to fight typical cognitive decline from age, illness, or trauma.

These activities help to summarize how we must keep alert to how we do things every day: challenge yourself intellectually, pursue diverse activities, focus on focusing, meditate daily, think about thinking, exercise with intensity/frequency, and keep balance in your life in every dimension.

Summary

A strong core is the starting point for being indispensable and empowering a successful career. You are the key to your future. Be physically fit so that your cognitive fitness is at its highest.

Establish habits that challenge yourself regularly. Be intense and passionate.

Do not let the internet dumb you down and distract you. Focus in 90-minute bursts of productivity throughout the day.

Turn off those interrupt-driven electronics and applications to turn on your productivity.

Read books to learn but also to nurture key cognitive processes.

Make Yourself Indispensable

Communicate with effective parables; bridge extrema to reach your audience; draw pictures to build teams; and listen, learn, and write things down.

Now that you have strengthened your core success skills, we will examine how you should interact with others.

While you may be efficient and innovative, achieving career success will often require you to function as part of a team. You do not become a success by yourself, even though it starts with your skills, diligence, passion, and attitude.

B. INTERACT WITH OTHERS

The first rule of interacting with others is to treat everyone with the same level of respect and kindness. As a matter of fact, being honest, being kind, and trying your hardest are the only rules you really need to remember. If this sounds like advice you might have heard from the classic *How To Win Friends and Influence People* by Dale Carnegie, I would be proud. It is that tugging back to high touch qualities while we are being pummeled by high tech solutions that will distinguish you from the crowd.

> "Be honest, be kind, and do your best."

Are you the only one who sends a written thank you note for a job well done by a member of your team and do you walk down to the contract specialist when there is a question on your recently opened contract rather than sending an impersonal e-mail? If you said "yes" to both, you are uniquely relating to others!

Make Yourself Indispensable

There are some specific issues that you should be attuned to for the three potential interactions you can have: with subordinates, with peers, and with bosses. When we discuss how you interact with your bosses, do not forget when you are the boss how you would like to be treated and let your people know. You really need to be a leader when you interact with your peers, subordinates, and bosses.

A leader, in any capacity, is usually not best served by sitting at the head of the table and barking orders; sometimes the most influential and powerful leader is one who can lead *from* the pack. Before detailing the attributes of an innovative leader, I will first introduce the innovation compass: a valuable framework for interacting with others and your environment.

Everyone Needs a Guide Star

To be agile in building your career, you must be able to move in any direction to react to obstacles (which are often people) and still navigate to your final objective. The innovation compass is an intuitive foundation for effective and efficient deliberations. The four directions are the same as the cardinal points of a compass: north, south, east, and west.

The east-west directions are consistent with thinking like an easterner *(holistic, unifying themes, and embracing of continuous approaches)* or thinking like a westerner *(linear and using categorization to solve)*.

These span the spectrum of how one logically assembles information. Neither approach is better in an absolute sense; they are just different. Which one is most appropriate depends on the situation. To achieve career success, you must appreciate and apply techniques at either extreme.

Many Easterners cannot understand the "part" without understanding the "whole." They search for relationships between things rather than trying to group problems (by categorizing) as Westerners often are inclined to do.

> "Eastern thought focuses on unifying themes while Western thinkers try to categorize issues and problems."

Easterners often prefer compromise solutions and holistic arguments; they are also more willing to endorse both of two apparently contradictory arguments. Generally, when someone

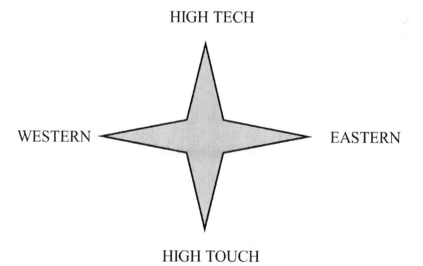

HIGH TECH

WESTERN — EASTERN

HIGH TOUCH

does this we may think that they are trying to deceive us. However, they are merely reflecting their appreciation for flexibility (in advance).

The north-south continuum describes how one acts and is consistent with the high tech *(tools, algorithms, what, computation, implementation)* and high touch *(communications, how, trust, bridger)* extremes. These disparate perspectives must also be embraced and used when most applicable, depending upon the conditions.

To take the wheel of your career and deftly navigate around potholes using both high tech and high touch foci at the right times and right places is crucial.

> "To be successful you need to use a balance of high tech and high touch techniques at the right times and in right places."

Each person and each team needs to have the openness to embrace these four ideals to prepare for any challenge or achieve any objective. If you are the leader and you do not have members with these skills that create "motion" in all four directions then you must be able to role play and act in these dimensions to avoid psychological inertia pulling you to the "safe solution" that may be a cognitive trap.

Often, some of the skills (e.g., willing to embrace new ideas) are needed most at the beginning of a project, such as during the concept exploration stage, and then different ones (e.g., methodically examining requirement satisfaction) are needed later during the implementation phase.

Similarly, a single worker may be challenged in the morning to apply high tech capabilities but then in the afternoon need high touch skills. The productive worker (i.e., indispensable) is able to do both. If a person is one-dimensional either way, all of the time, there will be a shortfall at some point. The capability and inclination to use a particular balance of skills depends on one's upbringing, education, work experience, and situational context.

Eastern thought focuses on unifying themes and belief in constant change, with the world always moving back to some prior state. This equilibrium appreciates the middle ground that Western thinkers often consider to be a compromising of values.

The innovation compass metaphor was developed not just due to the symmetry of orthogonal dimensions of "how" to execute but also because a compass is used to go places – a better, more successful future.

The innovation compass has a third dimension: intensity. This is nominally inversely proportional to the duration of the activity. I will use running analogies since they are fairly universally understood.

Some people are sprinters and some people are long distance runners. Both extremes (and many paces in between) are needed from time to time depending upon the challenge at hand. Usually, a sprinter executes at a fast pace for a short distance, exploding when needed, and then resting. Conversely, a marathoner maintains a steady pace for hours. Runners consider the mile one of the most difficult races because it is basically a long distance sprint, a painful combination.

We all have to deal with the same tradeoffs. Sometimes, we need to work on a proposal day and night for a week or study for a final exam. It hurts, but it is worth it in the end.

Routinely, it is best to work at a reasonable pace that you can keep up for a long time without collapsing uselessly in your office or lab but also having the versatility to sprint a short distance when needed.

The speed of action and pace of interaction cannot be considered without examining social media. Applications such as Facebook and Twitter create effective means to stay connected with business colleagues, loved ones, the news media, and other

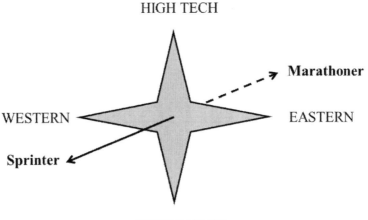

critical dimensions of one's life. As a result, these tools provide a way to rapidly communicate with many people very quickly.

However, they do not provide the richness of personal dialogue (high touch) necessary to establish or enrich relationships. You might be able to maintain existing personal, technical, and business relationships that were created the old-fashioned way, talking face-to-face. Yet, I propose that you cannot *establish* these enduring relationships on-line. The problem is that there is no operating manual for social media or personal relationships; it is often just trial and error.

> "Social media is great for maintaining enduring relationships but not for establishing them."

It is likely that having three short face-to-face meetings with team members is superior to sending one blanket e-mail. It may be less efficient in content delivery but will be more effective long-term because you will see the body language, hear the tone of voice, and sense the general level of understanding.

In summary, the majority of people problems for any age are not addressed optimally through social media, including e-mails. Recent research by the Harvard Business School highlighted the importance of face-to-face (i.e., high touch) interactions as being critical to effective team collaboration that in turn lead to future innovations. (Boufreau, Ganglui, Gaule, Guinan, & Lakhani, 2012)

Make Yourself Indispensable

Now that I have described the construct and utility of the innovation compass, let's examine the larger context of leadership as a key dimension of interacting with others.

Always Be a Leader

One oft-quoted definition of leadership is "a process of social influence in which one person can enlist the aid and support of others in the accomplishment of a common task." (Chemers, 1997) However, I have developed a new definition for leadership that I find more compelling:

> "Leadership is the skill that one wields to rally the members of an organization to behave in such a way, individually and collectively, to empower them to meet organizational objectives short-term and long-term."

It is important to note that leaders find themselves in a range of operational situations which I categorize as routine (*basic operations*), change agent (*significant performance changes required of the organization*), and emergency (*highly stressful, potentially life-threatening or disastrous environment*).

All of the leadership skills are required for this range of operational environments though the way leaders use their leadership skills differ. It is also true that not all leaders are good in all of these situations; some leaders excel in only one type of situation. General George Patton is a great example of someone

Make Yourself Indispensable

who was an effective leader in battle (i.e., emergency) but was not a great leader in peacetime (i.e., routine).

Before describing the specific skills required of you to be seen as a leader (even when you are not in charge) it is useful to note that the context of the situation drives the relative emphasis of the skills needed. The team context includes people in the team or organization, external conditions, and internal conditions.

The skills required of an "innovative leader" fall within three dimensions: thinking, communicating, and making/running teams.

Thinking includes an ability to (1) learn relevant skills (*e.g., accounting, engineering, and marketing*), (2) to avoid cognitive biases in decision making (*e.g., discriminating between relevant and irrelevant information*), (3) to focus on constant learning as a priority, and (4) to apply mature thought processes (i.e., *reacting responsibly to the action of others and not jumping to conclusions without all of the information*).

Communicating is important because it creates the means for the leader to interact with other members of the organization. Communication includes showing respect, listening, expressing complex concepts in simple ways (such as parables and pictures), and tailoring approaches real-time in response to context (including internal and external factors).

A leader must generate trust and provide clarity. Never criticize people; instead, criticize the processes by which others operate, so you do not make an issue personal.

> "Never criticize people. Criticize the processes
> by which they operate."

The ability to *make and run teams* builds on the first two
dimensions (thinking and communicating) but also requires a
deliberate intent to empower, not force, performance; embraces
cognitively diverse team membership; and infuses passion and
energy into team operations.

In summary, a leader must be the catalyst for team performance,
not the engine. This is the theme for all interactions with others:
your presence should help everyone else perform better.

> "Leaders are catalysts, not the engine;
> conductors, not the orchestra. Your presence
> should help everyone else perform better."

The concept of the "flux" leader, introduced in Fast Company
(Safian, 2012), suggests that the new global business
environment is putting an ever greater importance on being able
to respond to context changes, possibly as frequently as every
three months – a much faster pace in momentum swings than
ever before. They also highlight the need to be able to handle a
large range of business issues such as efficiency vs openness and
thrift vs ambition.

However, the changing context not only increases the need to
respond better to changing situations but also reinforces the

importance of sharpening your thinking skills. As discussed previously, you must be able to absorb a wide variety of new content as problems get increasingly complex, global, and interrelated. (Costa, 2012)

Author Rebecca Costa warns that in the future success will require people to think beyond current, traditional beliefs to solve the next generation of problems. She highlights the need to overcome cognitive biases and psychological inertia created by people thinking and acting consistently with the past and without enough focus on the future.

If we cannot continue to keep the complex problems of our future reduced to simple nested challenges, the complexity of the world will cause the quality of our decision making process to plummet.

My overall thesis is that to be seen as indispensable you must strive to be an "innovative leader": a leader who is strong in all three of basic leadership skills outlined earlier (thinking, communicating, and running teams) *and* perceptive enough to tailor one's approach to the ever changing context.

The primary "intangible" that the innovative leader provides, that other leaders may not care about as much, is trust. Trust within an organization produces higher morale, improved organizational loyalty, better delegation of authority, and more effective execution to enable strategy empowerment.

75

Make Yourself Indispensable

> "The primary "intangible" that an indispensable person provides is trust."

The primary actions within the framework of leadership skills that create this bond include knowledge sharing; deliberate actions of setting and meeting expectations; and hiring, rewarding, and firing the right people. These are all rooted in strong communication skills (i.e., transmitting and receiving). (Heskett, 2012)

Richard Branson has been mentioned by some as an exceptional modern industrial leader. He summarizes his leadership approach quite simply (Ankeny, 2012): "You definitely need to be good with people to help bring out the best in people. You need to be good at praising, and you need to be great at building a team and not trying to do everything yourself. You need to be able to not take all the credit for yourself, and you need to be able to take the knocks when things go wrong."

Becoming indispensable is not a zero sum game; you do not have to put down other people to reach your career goals. I cannot think of anyone who is closer to having a successful career than Richard Branson, yet he is not pounding on people to get or stay on top.

She Has a Presence About Her...

Being thoughtful and analytic is good, right? That is not always true, according to some research conducted at Stanford University. (Kupor, Tormala, & Norton, 2013) There appears to

76

be a "right" amount of thinking that a person should exhibit to earn others' respect, appreciation, and trust.

It probably is not a shock that if someone ponders which flavor of gum to purchase for ten minutes, others watching will consider that individual indecisive and, maybe even, ridiculous. However, it was found that people observe and act upon even subtle mismatches between the time spent on making a decision and the perceived complexity and importance of the posed problem.

The research showed that how someone evaluates a leader making a decision - any decision - will greatly affect how willing they will be to support and trust that person.

The situation where someone quickly makes a complex decision is seen as equally detrimental to engendering trust as over-analyzing a simple decision. An individual who is seen as spending the appropriate amount of time on a decision relative to its complexity and importance is considered "well-calibrated."

In addition, you must consider the relative differences of the observers' comfort level with snap decisions for critical topics or tedious analysis of simple decisions. Always consider the audience, even when you do not know you are being watched!

> "Do not overthink trivial problems or trivialize big problems."

However, one must wonder if you could deflect some of the judgment if an individual did some preparation before a decision

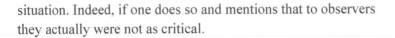

situation. Indeed, if one does so and mentions that to observers they actually were not as critical.

The most important take away about this dynamic is not that people categorize others for the level of effort going into a problem relative to the importance of the specific situation, but that they do so without even knowing it.

For this reason, as you are interacting with or near team members whom you wish to inspire and lead in the future, be sure to neither overthink simple situations or trivialize critical decisions. The pressure is on; everyone is watching and they *will* hold it against you!

Similarly, culture is not a byproduct of people you have in your organization but rather the actions that these people perform. It is often said that "you are what you do (or eat...)." Well, even more than that, you can actually convince yourself to be something you are not. For example, it has been shown that if you smile enough you will actually get happier. (Hanna, 2010) So, if you model behavior that shows respect, you can build a respectful culture, and so on.

> "Culture is a byproduct of actions performed by people in an organization."

Similarly, even standing in a way that appears to project power can make you feel more in control while the opposite is also true. A weak posture will make you feel less in control. In this way, action is not only about following corporate policy but also posturing (sometimes literally) in ways to attain personal satisfaction and goals.

Speaking of personal action, it has been shown that people who are warm and embracing of others in team environments are more effective in getting their team to perform. While you cannot be completely incompetent, exhibiting warmth and passion for the goals of the organization and compassion for others are more important than competence in getting a team to follow you and execute.

Haven't you been angry at some point in your career where you saw a person who did not know the problems or the solutions related to your organization as well as you, yet they were appointed to a leadership position that you wanted?

Upon reflection, you might find that that individual garnered the leadership position through appreciating other peoples' skills more than their own...

> "If you are warm and embracing of others in team environments you are more likely to be effective at leading a team to better performance."

Research has also shown that "lucky" people not only embrace their network of colleagues but also smile and make eye contact more than the average person. However, one might ask, are people "lucky" because they are more engaging or are they more engaging because they are "lucky?"

Make Yourself Indispensable

Studies show that "lucky" people were friendly and cooperative before the luck came their way. (Seelig, 2009)

Traceability

The key contribution as a member of a management team is the creation of behavior-based metrics that insure organizational performance. This transfer function is the primary job of leaders, if you cannot do this, then "go home."

Organizational performance is a huge enabler to your career and recognition, so it is important to understand what behaviors lead to group success. These behavior-based metrics are largely amplified in meetings as flash points in any organization's pulse or operational tempo. If you want to get a quick gauge of an organization's health, examine the number, length, and running of meetings.

When you run meetings, it is productive to start and end meetings with an eye on specific outcomes. One minute should be used as a meeting starts to explain what is hoped to be gained from the meeting. At the end of the meeting, the key action items should be reviewed. (Pullen, 2012)

If you regularly have nothing to do as a result of a recurring meeting you should question whether or not you should attend next time. The obvious exception is if the meeting is intended purely as an information distribution meeting. In that case, it is likely that a set of meeting minutes would have been sufficient for you to garner the information shared during the meeting.

Make Yourself Indispensable

However, just getting people together who routinely do not see each other may bring value in renewing personal relationships or triggering topics of joint interest.

If it is common that people have their smartphones or laptops out early and often during a meeting, there are only two possibilities: 1) the meeting is a round-robin event where people are not expected to listen or participate until it is their time to contribute or 2) the meeting is not bringing enough value to the participants and the meeting needs to have fewer people, happen less often, be shorter, or all of these.

I used to have "huddles" in a common area for action meetings when I ran a 30-person division; my key managers and I stood, discussed, and moved on in 15 minutes. When having any meeting, have a clear, limited objective and get it done!

Now is a good time to talk about a specific type of meeting often chartered in the name of productivity and innovation: the brainstorming session. A brainstorming meeting is much more productive when participants build lists of ideas and potential metrics before getting together in a group.

When the meeting is preceded by private brainstorming homework, more and better ideas result. Not only do active participants contribute more, but individuals who probably would not participate in group brainstorming sessions will make contributions by their written input.

Make Yourself Indispensable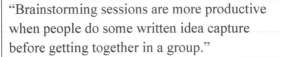

> "Brainstorming sessions are more productive when people do some written idea capture before getting together in a group."

There are three practical behaviors for the general workplace environment that are traceable to enhanced performance: encourage, focus, and enrich.[8]

Encourage: How many positive statements are made by leaders (relative to negative statements) about peers, subordinates, or the organization? By the way, many small, simple positive gestures are better than one large celebration. You can do this by trying to "catch people doing things right."

A recent study reported that, for highly productive teams, the positive to negative feedback ratio was 5:1 while for low-performing teams it was 1:2. ("Why Appreciation Matters", 2012) As stated earlier, you should praise diligence or effort, not intelligence or talent. Praising can be done simply by saying "thank you" and by including some positive body language; it need not be a large cash award or trophy.

Focus: People work better when they are not continually required to switch tasks. As stated earlier, 90 minutes is the optimal time for a single concentrated task. A "focus" metric is the amount of time during a day in which one stays focused on a

---

[8] The suite of metrics is partially adapted from an article by James Slavet of Greylock Partner.
http://www.forbes.com/sites/bruceupbin/2011/12/13/five-new-management-metrics-you-need-to-know/

single task without interruption divided by the hours in the work day.

For example, if an employee worked 90 minutes on a paper then spent 30 minutes catching up on e-mails, making phone calls, and other quick tasks then repeated that four times throughout the day for an eight hour day they would score a whopping 75% (i.e., 6hrs/8hrs).

Let your people breathe and think! Even if it is difficult to change your work environment, you must try to nudge it in the right direction. For example, one might impose a "no meeting Friday" rule to give an organization some leeway and inspiration in this area.

Enrich: Enriching others is a critical dimension for any employee. We define how much value (V) someone gets from an interaction with you divided by the amount of energy or effort (E) they had to put into the interaction as the V/E ratio.

You should strive for a high V/E ratio in all of your interactions. The difficulty here is that the individual you are dealing with actually defines both V and E so you must listen and pay attention to what is important to them in order to "score well."

> "Strive for a high V/E ratio in all of your interactions."

Never be afraid to contribute to a group activity – any group or any activity! Know what you know and know what you don't know. Even serving as the straight-man, asking basic expository questions can be critical.

Make Yourself Indispensable

You can be "brilliant in your ignorance" because you are not afraid of being wrong and, as such, you will probably act as a spark for better understanding for all. Different perspectives always challenge a team of people to adapt their own skills and tools more craftily to the team challenge.

It is not just a hunch that a group of people actually makes better decisions than a monolithic team. The Diversity Prediction Theorem states that the predictive capability of a team is determined equally by the quality of the individuals and the diversity in their backgrounds. (Page, 2011)

This means that a more diverse group, with moderately smart people, will outperform a single brilliant person. As a result, a meeting slated for establishing future key actions is better if there is a little disagreement; this diversity in opinion hints at a better eventual outcome. (Page, 2011) Immediate consensus is fool's gold!

> "Immediate consensus is fool's gold!"

Some Things Never Get Old

All throughout this book I discuss balance...balance between eastern and western thinking, balance between tools and techniques, and so on. When it comes to interpersonal relationships, the "high touch" is valuable and should not be overwhelmed by the "high tech."

Make Yourself Indispensable

One of the archetypical sources of valuable people skills was written nearly 80 years ago. In examining *How to Win Friends and Influence People*, Dale Carnegie prescribed a series of direct and indirect behaviors that have stood the test of time. They are listed in the table below. (Carnegie, 1936, 1981)

Carnegie did not focus on complicated rules; his rules are simple and ageless but profound. His tenets are steeped in personal activities that anyone can perform easily; it is not rocket science.[9] Positive intent and kindness were his calling cards, not imposing of wills and crafting of directives.

Interacting With Others: Best Practices	
Indirect	Direct
- Call attention to people's mistakes indirectly. - Let the other person save face. - Give the other person a fine reputation to live up to. - Make the other person happy about doing the thing you suggest.	- Begin with praise and honest appreciation. - Talk about your own mistakes before criticizing the other person. - Ask questions instead of giving direct orders. - Praise the slightest improvement and praise every improvement. Be lavish in your praise. - Use encouragement. Make the fault seem easy to correct.

Dealing with Bosses

Bosses are like anybody else, time is their most important asset. Either save them time (by being proactive and solving problems

---

[9] ...And I know, because I am a rocket scientist!

before they materialize) or, at a minimum, do not waste their time.

You should strive for all of your interactions to have a high V/E ratio, but especially with your boss.

It is also critical not to "sugar-coat" discussions. A good boss does not want to take 15 minutes to hear a 30-second issue that you are waffling about.

Most important, if you have a problem with your organization or your boss, talk directly to your boss; speak up, not out. That is to say, go "up" your chain of command, not "out" to anyone who will listen. Do not complain to people about an issue they cannot solve.

> "Speak up… not out! Do not complain to people about an issue they cannot solve."

Do not criticize a bad boss to your peers. Be loyal to people in their absence. Others will begin having more faith and confidence in you because they know that you won't be talking about them behind their backs. (Stephen Covey interview, 2012)

Responsiveness is more important than quality. This is true, though a little counter-intuitive. Responsiveness trumps quality if you use creating an early version of a document to receive feedback that will eventually make the document or product better and to show the receiver that you take the assignment seriously.

Make Yourself Indispensable

Summary

Before moving on to the final dimension of career success, investing in your future, we need to review the critical aspects of interacting with others.

Organizations do not perform, people do! Therefore, it is critical to your professional and personal success to be astute in your dealings with people.

Be honest, be kind, and do your best.

Do not just react to the world. Be proactive, make others react to you. Save time of others around you.

Do not listen passively. Listen with positive intent to understand the speaker's content *and* context. Be a keynote listener; this is the only way to progress in knowledge. Show respect by taking notes and synthesizing before interrupting.

Never forget that people remember how you make them feel more than they recall the facts you shared.

Your passion and enthusiasm are always the lingering differentiators after interacting with others.

Speak up... not out! Do not complain to people about an issue they cannot solve.

Make Yourself Indispensable

Believe it or not, it is most important to be responsive. Give people early drafts, give time for feedback, and show that you are listening.

If people do not feel more energized or better off after interacting with you, they probably will not fight to have you back and, definitely, will not consider you indispensable.

C. INVEST IN YOUR FUTURE

The last dimension of becoming indispensable is the most difficult to implement because it requires time and patience: investing in your future. A large part of investing in your future is to develop and execute a strategy.

Understanding how to develop an effective strategy is important for two reasons. First, career success is only achieved through the implementation of a coherent strategy or plan. Second, you will be a more valuable employee if you are able to contribute to or lead strategic planning efforts.

> "Understanding how to develop an effective strategy is important for executing on your own career strategy and for assisting on your organization's strategy."

Strategy cannot be created, refined, or executed without a clearly articulated challenging objective in mind. The goal assumed by this book is that you want to become indispensable and strive to have a successful career. As I said before, your innovation compass is only useful if you know where you are going and why you want to go there.

Yes. I am going to say the "A-word": ambition. Ambition is not bad as long as you adhere to all of the previous advice. Without ambition, a person is adrift.

Follow the Light...

The framework developed for enduring organizational productivity includes individual actions, team activities, and organizational policies synchronizing to create enhanced performance. Wise, mature, and knowledgeable employees are assembled into teams to enable productive and sustainable operations.

Strategy is the cohesive set of actions that anchors the interaction between the three levels of the organization. Strategy is all about action; actions are performed by individuals and based on clarity of purpose that is created through personal interactions that are traceable to a challenging objective.

Good strategy is simple, though it is not easy to develop, express, and execute. (Rumelt, 2011)

Strategy is not a synonym for innovation but it might well produce innovation across all levels of an organization. Hoped-for outcomes are part of the context of a strategy but they are not the substance of a strategy.

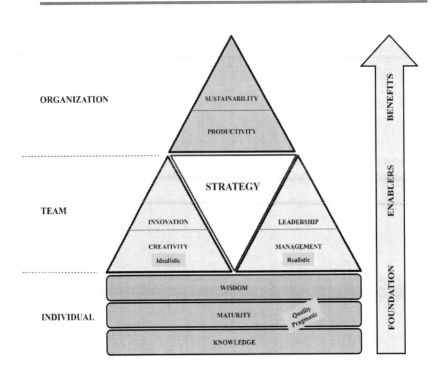

Strategy defines a path around, through, and over obstacles. If you do not know the topography of challenges then you cannot create the success path.

An important aspect of a strategy is determining the primary hurdles to achieving your objective and crafting ways to best overcome them to attain a goal. This path includes coordinated analyses, concepts, policies, arguments, and actions to counter challenges. Action, as always, is the key! These actions are traceable from organizational challenges to individual behaviors.

Make Yourself Indispensable

A step often omitted is the identification and documentation of all possible levers available to an organization to execute a strategy. Without a conscious effort to do this, strategy teams do not examine the full spectrum of possible means to overcome obstacles to achieve the goal.

For businesses, levers may include labor rates, overhead, benefits, and location of offices while for an academic environment they may include class sizes, number of athletic teams, and student transportation costs.

Without a review of the levers, it will just be assumed that previous actions are the type of activities that can considered in a new strategy. Yet, this will most likely be very constraining.

Actions that do not propel you down the "path" more efficiently should not be undertaken; good strategies include saying "no" to certain tasks.

In summary, the strategy development process has four key steps:

1. Set challenging organizational outcome(s);
2. Identify and characterize obstacles to attaining the outcome(s);
3. Identify all possible levers to help attain the outcome(s); and
4. Document specific traceable actions to overcome the obstacles in pursuit of the desired outcome(s).

A strategy is the set of specific traceable actions, not the desired outcomes. It is a call to arms and an execution roadmap, not a lot of empty promises.

> "Strategy is the set of specific traceable actions, not the desired outcome(s)."

Bad strategy normally focuses only on performance and never addresses problems. You can usually detect bad strategy by the use of flowery language, statements of high ambition, lists of desired outcomes, and vision statements while neglecting to identify or address key challenges.

The worst strategy mistake, but also the most common one, is not to have a strategy at all. Again, this is just as critical for an individual career: with no career strategy, the likelihood of success is small.

A great example of effective strategy development dealt with the Cold War. (Rumelt, 2011) Andy Marshall, head of the Office of Net Assessment, was tasked with figuring out a strategy to defeat the Soviets in the 1970s. While the majority of people at that time focused on Mutual Assured Destruction (MAD), Mr Marshall (with James Roche) developed a different approach.

They noted an economic weakness of the Soviet Union, so they focused on the U.S. developing systems (such as the Strategic Defense Initiative, SDI) that would be costly for the Soviets to counter and contribute nothing to their offensive capability.

This was contrary to the escalating arms race under the moniker of MAD, the prevailing strategy at the time, but it describes exactly what happened – trying to keep up with SDI crippled the Soviet economy.

> "Good strategy works by focusing energy and resources on one, or a very few, pivotal actions or behaviors whose accomplishment will lead to a cascade of favorable outcomes."

Even after you establish a sound strategy, the situation may change. It becomes critical to know when to shift strategies instead of keeping "true" to an established strategy. Objective and regular assessment of progress toward a goal will provide the insight needed to know when to adapt rather than execute.

Being conversant in strategy development, planning, and execution is a valuable part of your skill set that will make you a valuable contributor - maybe even indispensable - to any organization and, as such, will contribute to your career success.

> "Being conversant in strategy development, planning, and execution will contribute to your career success."

Compound Interest

You must invest in your career growth. Investing means to "devote one's time, effort, or energy to a particular undertaking with the expectation of a worthwhile result." (Henderson, 2008) This is exactly what pursuing career success is about!

Make Yourself Indispensable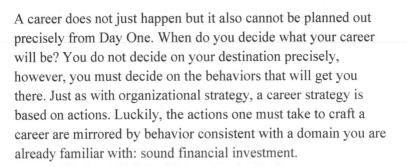

A career does not just happen but it also cannot be planned out precisely from Day One. When do you decide what your career will be? You do not decide on your destination precisely, however, you must decide on the behaviors that will get you there. Just as with organizational strategy, a career strategy is based on actions. Luckily, the actions one must take to craft a career are mirrored by behavior consistent with a domain you are already familiar with: sound financial investment.

I am sure that you have been told to deposit money in your Independent Retirement Account (IRA) early and let compound interest do much of the work for you. It takes deliberate action that requires sacrifice decades before you will benefit.

The same is true with your career. While others are spending all of their spare time on leisure activities, start investing in your career by learning a new skill, meeting with an extra business acquaintance, or documenting key insights.

Anything that both increases your capabilities and exposes you to new domains will be a strong base for growth. It is never too early or too late to get started. Begin investing 5% of your discretionary leisure time (about 30 minutes a day) into building new capabilities and the benefits will start to accrue fairly quickly.

You will get there faster if you commit 10%!

> "Treat your career like an IRA; make deposits early and regularly."

Make Yourself Indispensable

When the internet bubble burst in 2000, many people lost everything because they had invested ravenously in the immediate winner, but they lost their investment balance. Just as diversity creates robustness in physical systems, so does it in career advancement.

Take jobs that are the equivalent of mutual funds with a balance between compensation, skills development, training opportunities, convenience, benefits, and mentoring networks.

As your portfolio matures, so will your career. You learn, build competence, make trusted colleagues, and incrementally map your way to your destination of becoming indispensable!

Be versatile but avoid being a "jack of all trades and a master of none." Whatever you do; do it well, do your best. However, do not be afraid to take excursions periodically into other domains and specialties to keep aware of diverse techniques and thought processes. Bringing these new methods back to your primary field of interest keeps you fresh and unique.

When determining just how hard you are going to work to make your career soar, think about the Chinese bamboo tree. The gardener prepares the soil, plants the bulbs, and tends to the area for four years.

During this time, all of the growth is in the roots underground. Nothing can be seen above the ground but the bamboo tree is patiently growing an efficient root system, a strong foundation for future growth. In the fifth year, the bamboo tree grows up to 80 feet.

Make Yourself Indispensable

By the way, it is nearly impossible to kill or eliminate bamboo once it has matured. Model your career development after the bamboo plant; nurture critical skills and your network of professionals early, then exercise patience while they coalesce into a powerful framework for future career success.

> "Model your career development after the bamboo plant to empower your future career success."

Fine Line Between Success and Failure

A critical enabler of career success is happiness. You heard me right - happiness. The people who try to do something that they hate, because their parents told them to or a magazine said they would get paid well, are usually miserable. You have seen and heard that most successful people are happy. Why is that?

Are they happy because they are successful or were they successful first and then they became happy?

My observation is that unhappy people rarely become successful. They drag others down. Their unhappiness is perceived as a lack of commitment, they are not singled out for collaborative opportunities, and they do not put in the extra time into their career development.

> "Unhappy people rarely become successful."

Make Yourself Indispensable

So how do you determine the career that will make you happy and successful in pursuing? First, you must figure out three things:

- NEED: In what skills and expertise do you need to be proficient for your chosen career?
- SKILL: What are you good at? What things do people envy about your ability to do faster and better than anyone else?
- PREFERENCE: What do you like to do? Left to your own devices, what would you do if you had six hours free on the weekend?

If you were to fill out a table showing your existing skills, you would start by listing your talents along the y-axis as a function of competency (i.e., skill level) with the best at the top and worst at the bottom.

Next, move them across the x-axis as a reflection of how much you like (i.e., preference) to do these tasks. The activities that you like the most you move further along the x-axis.

This gives you a useful depiction of your likely career stress or blessing since if you are bad at things that you like it is not a comfortable situation.

Lastly, bold the items that you think you have to be able to do well in order to achieve success in your career. If you have lots of bolded entries in the lower left hand quadrant (i.e., dislike and poor skill level for needed skills) you have a lot of work to do.

Make Yourself Indispensable

You can build a Skills Assessment Table to represent these three dimensions: preference, skill level, and need. The Skills Assessment Table below shows the depiction of my "skills fingerprint."

		Dislike	Neutral	Love
SKILL LEVEL	Expert	**Managing People; Running Meetings**	Business Development; **Making Viewgraphs**	**Technology Evaluation; Research and Development; Modeling; Public Speaking; Technical Writing**
	Average	Organizing Information Databases; Financial Tracking of Projects	**Mentoring People; Proposal Writing; Managing Programs**	Creative Writing; Sports; **Simulation**
	Poor	Software Coding	Mathematical Proofs	Music; Operations Research
SKILLS ASSESSMENT (Bold "Needed" Skills)		Dislike	Neutral	Love
		PREFERENCE		

I am fairly far along in my career so it is not surprising that my Skills Assessment Table shows a great consistency in preference, skill level, and need (i.e., many bolded entries in the upper right-hand quadrant). Early in my career, I wanted to grow a team of people because I perceived that management responsibility was a measure of my contribution to the organization.

However, over time I found that I could not be both an expert technologist and a good personnel manager. As a result, I started to ask for jobs where I had no one working for me so that I could focus on performing technology development efforts at an expert level.

It may have affected my salary and bonuses at the time but eventually the Chief Technology Officer and Chief Scientist skills became more relevant to organizations for which I worked. Therefore, I had aligned what I liked to do with what I was good at and, as a bonus, it was what the companies needed. The last 15 years have been incredibly productive as I have continually focused and aligned my skills, aided largely by my self-imposed annual résumé reviews (more on this later).

Therefore, if you draw your Skills Assessment Table, you will find that there are probably three things you might have to do: (1) love stuff that you are good at, (2) get better at things you love to do, and (3) align your career aspirations with things that you are both proficient in and enjoy.

The problem is that some of these are quite hard and require effort to enable each of these processes. The difference between success and failure (making your career composed of things you prefer and at which you are proficient) is in habits, listening, and luck.

> "The difference between success and failure is in habits, listening, and luck."

Let's deal with these in reverse order.

Luck. Every successful person had some luck yet it is hard to tell you how to generate luck but suffice it to say that luck will not come knocking on your door. It almost always happens while you are working hard with other people with positive intent while your "unlucky" peers are watching TV or on Facebook.

This brings us to the second factor: listening. I have already covered listening but the importance of this skill cannot be overestimated. You need to listen to others and listen to yourself. What do other people love about you? How do you make people feel when you always get your final reports in early, giving people time to review leisurely, rather than under a tight time schedule?

Listening is often the first step in learning which is critical to becoming indispensable. Listen to yourself; what do *you* enjoy doing and do more of that. The difficulty comes when people tell you that they love an aspect of your job that you hate. Or they think you must add a dimension to your professional skills that you are not good at doing. Then what? Reacting to these challenges is where the third key to success comes in: habits.

"Habits" sound so boring, how could this help develop a career? Well, the only way to change a behavior is to create a habit. A habit is formed by a sequence of actions in sufficient frequency and intensity that you continue it without prompting (or even thinking). This definition is at the root of career success.

As discussed earlier, people become an expert at tasks when they execute deliberate practice with ever-increasing challenging goals along the way. If you want to change your situation by increasing your competency at a critical skill or convincing yourself that a skill you are good at is worth doing long-term, you have to work at it.

> "A habit is formed by a sequence of actions in sufficient frequency and intensity so it is likely that you will continue it without prompting (or even thinking)."

It is important to me that I am physically fit because it gives me more energy to work during the day, to look the role of a

Make Yourself Indispensable

competent scientist, and to enhance my cognitive capabilities, as discussed earlier.

I work out every week day and once on the weekend. I do this by making it the first thing that I do every day, so that extended meetings or delayed flights will not affect my workout schedule. It has become a habit.

In addition, I decided years ago that I enjoyed writing and felt it would provide a career differentiator but I was only average at it. As a result, I knew that I needed to work on that skill.

What did I do? I started reading books and writing book reports for colleagues and clients. This monthly book report was free to people and provided a regular, challenging activity for me to accomplish to hone my content synthesis and writing skills.

These book reports provided components of the book I published in 2011, *Hitting the Innovation Jackpot*. The book reports eventually morphed into my monthly *Cognovation Dialogues* essay that laid the groundwork for much of this book.

However, it also has permitted me to contribute more regularly to technical journals, corporate newsletters, and strategic planning off-sites.

Just as it is a fine line between success and failure, there is also a fine line between discipline and obsession. So, when have you become obsessed with a habit and when is it a disciplined practice? People can be obsessed with physical fitness. Am I obsessed because I work out every weekday morning at 4:45am?

Make Yourself Indispensable

The line between discipline and obsession occurs when the action that you are doing becomes more important than the benefit that it provides to a balanced lifestyle. I work out to feel good and be better at what I do on the job and with my family.

If my workouts start to become two hours in length and prevent me from getting my work done or following through on family commitments, exercise would be an obsession. It would be a habit that no longer provided the benefit that it was put in place to create.

There is that issue again - balance. People who are considered indispensable have balance. They balance family and work; they balance exercise and diet; they balance household chores and leisure activities; and they balance making money and being happy.

> "People who are considered indispensable have balance."

Summary

As we look for the "perfect job," never forget that there is no perfect job. There is a job that permits you to balance your skills, your needs, and your desires. That is as close as you can get to perfect.

Changing jobs is a major effort, however, you know you have to leave when you are not learning, not improving skills, not meeting new people, and not broadening your horizons. It should be about you, not about other people in your organization. There are incompetent people in every organization, so base your

Make Yourself Indispensable

decision about leaving a job on your career progression, not the state of others.

Do not be a job-hopper! A good rule of thumb is that you are not really productive in a job or organization until you have been there for 18 months. Many people make a snap decision about a job – give any job at least two years so you have some time at full capacity before making a job decision.

Now we have addressed the three dimensions of career success: a strong core, ability to interact positively with others, and taking a strategic view of your future. If you are doing all of these things and your current job situation does not allow you to improve your career status, it may be time to look elsewhere.

However, as you get farther up in the pecking order of an organization, your ability to progress is partly a function of the quality of the management team. There is even a personality to a senior management cadre; it is either good for you or it is not.

You know that you are in trouble when your management team looks like the cast of the Wizard of Oz...

> "You know that you are in trouble when your management team looks like the cast of the Wizard of Oz."

It might be hard for you to believe but many people are actually afraid of being a success. They begin to realize (either consciously or subconsciously) that they may have to take on more of a management role to continue to rise through the ranks in their organization. They may be unfamiliar and uncomfortable working in this capacity so they sabotage themselves and focus only on the liabilities of career advancement while ignoring the benefits. This often is realized by a plateauing of job responsibilities.[10]

However, most executive management will listen to exceptional performers and craft an upwardly mobile position that benefits both the employee and the organization. However, you have to be proactive and communicate your desires that make it a win for the organization. If all that fails, we can prepare you for getting a new job.

Yet, depending upon your personality and your industry, you might decide to create a company and be your own boss. While the rest of the book may not be as relevant if you are not a job-searcher, it will provide some valuable insights from an employer perspective if you are starting your own business.

In addition, starting your own company makes the first part of the book even more important; being considered indispensable will assist you in striking out on your own.

Transition to Roger

Roger is now going to take over this discussion. He reads more résumés in a year than I have read in my entire career. He has

---

[10] From a conversation with Bob Mitchell, Managing Partner, Executive Leadership Services LLC, July 2014.

Make Yourself Indispensable

seen literally the good, the bad, and the ugly when it comes to résumés.

If you have to change jobs to help propel your career forward then you will get some useful advice in the rest of this book.

Hopefully, you have internalized how to build a strong core of productivity, fine-tuned your people skills, and have adopted a strategic outlook to your career.

You should not have to use this advice on getting a new job very often. If you are changing jobs every few years, you are not paying attention to the book up to this point!

> "If you are changing jobs every few years, you are not paying attention to the book up to this point!"

A Little Perspective from Roger

Darren has, in the preceding pages, put together a very strong argument on how and why you need to stay on top of your career and what you need to do to be ready for a job change.

My mission is to educate you about some of the tools you need to make yourself visible, attractive, and prepared for getting your next job. Networking, creating a compelling résumé, getting your résumé into the right hands, interviewing, and following-up to an interview are important steps in this process.

Make Yourself Indispensable

> "Five steps to getting a new job are networking, creating a compelling résumé, distributing your résumé, interviewing, and follow-up to an interview."

I have been in the human capital business (i.e., human resources) for nearly 40 years, interviewing thousands of candidates from entry level to senior executive. This experience has taught me what works and what does not work in getting the right attention of recruiters and hiring managers.

My career in the human capital business is that of a generalist. I have some level of experience and expertise in all aspects of human capital management. This includes workforce planning, job analysis, talent management, on-boarding, off-boarding, benefits, employee services, strategic planning, recruitment, staffing, reductions-in-force, assessments, and career planning.

The part of the human capital business I liked the most, and still do today, is the talent piece; searching for and finding the very best talent for organizations to hire. I refer to it as precision hiring. Basically, it requires sitting down with hiring managers and asking a series of questions to get them to describe, in the most detail possible, their ideal candidates.

Your job as a candidate is to develop a résumé that clearly spells out your qualifications relative to the hiring organization so that you stand out and get the opportunity to compete for the job.

In the next section of this book, I explain the subtleties of the hiring process and advise you on your preparation for that eventual conversation about your next job.

Make Yourself Indispensable

Be aware of contextual changes to the job market. Global factors are affecting more and more jobs every day so be a student of worldwide business and culture even if you are looking for a job in Des Moines.

> "Global factors are affecting more and more jobs every day so be a student of worldwide business and culture."

The people I work with today who are out of work or stressed out because their industry is slowly being downsized all have said at one time or another that they wish they had taken the time to expand their knowledge base by taking an extra training course or learning a new skill. Had they followed Dr. McKnight's advice in the first part of this book, they would have been in a much better position to ride out a wave of double-digit unemployment.

Whether you need to change jobs to advance your career or have been laid off, there is a right way to go after your next job.

Make Yourself Indispensable

Make Yourself Indispensable

III. GETTING A NEW JOB

Earlier in the book Darren was very clear on changing jobs. You only change your job for a better opportunity and one that is going to advance your career.

> "You should only change your job if it is going to advance your career."

I had a client several years ago who requested my assistance to help him transition out of his current job into a new one. He believed he was underutilized in his current job and he saw no chance of promotion. He was struggling with both his performance and his interaction with his everyone in the company. After months of coaching from me, his performance and his attitude improved greatly. Today, he remains in the same job that he so wanted to leave years ago.

The purpose of this example is to demonstrate that in many cases, you can remain with your current company and find opportunities to contribute and expand your competencies.

Working harder or smarter in your current job will often lead to a promotion or greater job satisfaction. This in turn may indeed eliminate the need for leaving your current company. It is usually much easier to develop and grow in-place than to change jobs and disrupt your life with an uncertain return.

Most people leave their job because they dislike their bosses. Is that why you are leaving? Do you think you have outgrown your current situation and need a new company that will allow you to grow personally and professionally? Alternatively, is money driving your decision? Is the problem you? What are the typical reasons that people change jobs?

The top 10 reasons why people leave a job are listed below in reverse order with some of my thoughts about these reasons. (Carnegie, 2014)

10. The grass is greener on the other side – you hope but usually it is not the case.

9. Values do not align to the company – this is a crucial factor for happiness.

8. You don't feel valued – this is usually a perception vs. reality issue.[11]

7. Job insecurity – make sure that it is not your fault.

6. No room for advancement – this is critical if it is a part of your career plan to progress.

5. Unhappy with pay – this is not trivial but have you asked for a raise? Does your pay match industry standards?

4. Too much red tape – have you discussed with your boss why "red tape" is necessary?

3. Not being challenged – have you asked for more responsibility?

2. Passion is gone – this is your problem. Changing jobs probably will not help.

1. I hate my boss – this is very important; do you hate all of your bosses? If so, you might be the problem.

---

[11] However, perception is more important than reality!

Make Yourself Indispensable

> "The number one reason for people leaving their job is that they hate their boss but if you always hate your boss, it is probably your fault."

What is driving your decision to find a new job in your career journey? Once you are comfortable with the deficiency you are addressing then you are ready to begin the process. The process is not difficult but it requires planning and hard work. You must be able to articulate concisely why you are changing jobs because you will be asked often by various people throughout the process. Your reasoning must not insult your previous employer.

Before you go to all the trouble of changing jobs be sure that is what you need to do. Because when you change jobs you do more than change your job and you affect more than just yourself. It may change your 401K, your leave benefits, when you can take vacation, and your health plan. It may that be your spouse's favorite doctor is no longer a part of the new health plan.

While a new job will affect other people, getting that new job really is about how you prepare and execute a job search! Everything you do influences your possible move to a new position.

There are two things that are critical for you to do all of the time, not just in preparation of pursuing a new job: networking and building a compelling résumé. These two activities are part of sustaining a career.

Make Yourself Indispensable

We will cover these two activities first followed by distributing your résumé, interviewing, and following up from the interview. If you only network and look at your résumé right before you want to change jobs, you will probably be looking for a job for a long time. However, doing the upfront work of establishing and maintaining a vibrant network of professional colleagues in tandem with a current and compelling résumé will make your job search much more productive.

> "If you only network and look at your résumé right before you want to change jobs then you will likely be looking for a job for a long time."

Networking

In the old days, when unemployment hovered around 4%, most job seekers could find a new job in a matter of days. A résumé and a postage stamp were all you needed to get an interview and maybe a job offer. Newspapers had tens of pages of job opportunities and career fairs.

Today, the Washington Post Sunday classified section includes only a page or two of job openings and most of these require very special credentials. Many of these jobs have actually already been filled and they are only being advertised to meet the spirit of open competition for the position.

Most jobs, if advertised, are announced on job boards such as Monster, Indeed, Career Builder, USAJOBS, Cleared Jobs, etc. However, even with all the job boards and on-line job announcements on company-specific web sites, most jobs today are filled through networking.

Make Yourself Indispensable

You are encouraged to maintain and expand your network as a way of keeping current in your industry, paying forward by helping others, and continually learning. The other key benefit of networking comes when you are looking for a new job.

Thousands of job boards have been launched and there has been a rush of job seekers to find their dream job on the internet. However, the cost of advertising for new hires, either in news print or via a job board has become increasingly expensive.

As the cost of advertising for candidates continues to climb, employers have begun to incentivize their current workforce to help find talent. In recent years, the companies I have worked for have all had incentive programs for referring someone for hire to the company.

A typical policy is if the referred candidate is hired, the referring employee is given a bonus of as much as $7,000 – half paid after the new hire is on board for six months and the other half paid on the one-year anniversary of their employment.

You might think that is a lot of money for a company to pay for a referral. However, since current employees know what kind of person blends best into the company culture, this referral is low risk. The company knows an employee is not going to recommend someone for hire that they do not respect, believe would do a good job, and would be a nice addition to the team.

Referred employees tend to stay on the job because of the nice fit with the organization and the culture. Fewer bad hires save money through less employee turnover and less advertising. The cost of making a bad hire is estimated to be double the salary of that person.

> "The cost of making a bad hire is estimated to be double the salary of that person."

Therefore, you should be diligent about maintaining, and even expanding, your network during your career. However, once you decide to change jobs I suggest you execute this five-step network-leveraging sequence:

1. *List*: Make a list of all your friends, former coworkers, golfing buddies, tennis buddies, church associates, relatives, college buddies, parents of college buddies, neighbors, and professional association leadership who happen to be professionals in some capacity or another. The list should include the person's name, contact information, and why you think they could be helpful in your job search.

Once you think the list is complete, stop, put the list aside, and take your mind off your job search. Return to your list periodically and add to the list everyone you forgot to include on your initial list. You will be surprised how many people you add each time you work on the list.

One way to expand your network is to use professional social networks like LinkedIn to see who might be associated with a business area or company in which you are interested. You can sometimes reach out through your contacts to someone with the company who is a "friend of a friend" and they might respond to your request to connect.

I sometimes get "friend of a friend" connect requests on LinkedIn and have found that they can be a good way to expand my network. However, as always, be careful on social media. I do not accept requests from people who I do not know or I am not familiar with their company or industry.

Do not hound your network contacts. Use them in a professional way and they will be friends for life. Abuse the relationship and you will find that they probably will not respond to any e-mails or phone calls.

2. *Message*: Draft an e-mail that you can send to everyone; it should be fairly generic. However, it should also be direct and informative. The message should, as appropriate, remind the person how you know them and that you appreciate them taking the time to read your e-mail. What they do after that depends on how compelling a message you have written.

There is no need to explain why you are looking. You should state that you wanted to make the person aware of your circumstances in hopes that if they know of an opportunity or become aware of one in the future, that they will contact you.

You can attach a copy of your résumé or any collateral material you think would be useful as a way of reminding them who you are. Thank them for taking time to read your e-mail.

If you do not have an e-mail address you may have to make a

phone call and provide an abbreviated message in order to get an e-mail address to send along the résumé.

3. *Monitor*: Build a spreadsheet of everyone that you have reached out to and record the responses from your enquiries. You need to keep track of all correspondence. If you hear back from someone on the list, and it's a positive response, respond in turn with a big thank you and a request to have a conversation with the person as soon as possible. It could be your first step to a new position and the next chapter in your career. Even if they cannot help, thank them for their consideration.

4. *Targets*: In addition to making the list of contacts, begin to review the web sites of the companies that your network represents. Look for companies of interest and any vacancies you are eligible for and interested in. If it is a company of interest, make relevant notes about the company and what operational area is of particular interest. You are now in a position to hold an intelligent conversation about the company and maybe even a current opening.

5. *Act*: Look for networking opportunities, volunteer activities, professional meetings, conferences, job fairs, and university alumni gatherings. These are all opportunities to add to your network through face-to-face (i.e., high touch) interactions. Taking time out of your day for an hour visit with any one of these networking opportunities can be very helpful. Remember, you must invest in your career – this includes maintaining a vibrant network.

Make Yourself Indispensable

Networking Tips

Networking is not a one-time activity. It is something you need to start and maintain, even when you are not looking for a new job. You don't reach out to someone once. You plan and reach out multiple times as a way of making sure you are not forgotten. You never know when you might need their help and guidance.

Networking is not just about getting a new job. Networking is also a venue for you to mentor and be mentored. Having a senior person who you can bounce ideas off of while in an informal networking environment (e.g., over a cup of coffee or during an evening mixer) provides a great learning experience. As stated earlier, continual learning is a key attribute for becoming indispensable.

Regular networking with peers also provides a means to get smarter about your industry and garner intelligence on new opportunities. These meetings can be very rewarding and provide both new ideas and bursts of energy into your career pursuits.

How well you maintain and expand your network will have a large impact on your job search results; it is a two-way street. You are networking with others and they in turn will network with you (when they believe you can add value to their cause or provide valuable information). "Paying forward" with peers and colleagues is both tactically and strategically beneficial for your career development and job security, as we discussed earlier.

You must be incrementally active in your pursuit of career success. Every day, every week, every month you need to take

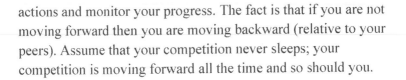

actions and monitor your progress. The fact is that if you are not moving forward then you are moving backward (relative to your peers). Assume that your competition never sleeps; your competition is moving forward all the time and so should you.

> "If you are not moving forward, you are moving backward. Deliberate activities are necessary to make progress. Success does not just happen."

Your career should not just have position. It should also have velocity and direction!

Building a Compelling Résumé

Just as you need to continually network, you need to continually update your résumé to ensure career success. It provides a means for assessing your progress and the résumé will be immediately available if you do make that decision to change jobs or just discuss your current career strategy.

The one universal fact is that a résumé must get the attention of the hiring manager and be ready when you need it! This is why we suggest that networking and maintaining a résumé should occur continually, even before you start looking for a new job.

We recommend that the résumé be built on what we call the "Four C's". It needs to be compliant, complete, coherent, and compelling.

Make Yourself Indispensable

Webster's dictionary defines these four words as follows.

Compliant – conforming to requirements

Complete – having all the necessary information

Coherent – being logical and organized, easy to understand

Compelling – able to capture and hold ones attention

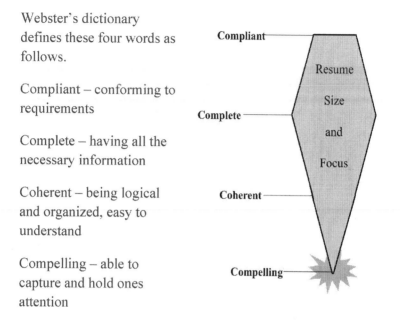

While we have four "C's," we suggest you execute the process in two steps:

1) compliant and complete – proper format and all potentially relevant information; and

2) coherent and compelling – refine the message to logically, concisely, and clearly state your value.

This process is relevant and useful for constructing any document, not just résumés.

Make Yourself Indispensable

Compliant and Complete – The Basics

First, your résumé needs to be compliant. Your credentials should be presented in a traditional résumé format and with the content that best describes your qualifications and competencies.

There are two basic résumé formats: 1) chronological or 2) functional. However, I have seen some résumés that are a hybrid of the two.

If you want the focus of the résumé to be on how you have acquired and demonstrated a particular skill or competency in which a hiring manager is interested, a functional résumé could be the best option. The functional résumé will highlight your abilities rather than your chronological work history. You'll still need to summarize your work history, but it is the secondary focus of the résumé.

If you want to explain how your career has evolved in logical steps then a chronological format would be best. Showing the most recent information first provides a way to highlight your latest accomplishments. This is by far the most popular format.

A final résumé should not exceed two pages in length but in the early stages of building your résumé do not worry about the length; it will get condensed when we focus on it being coherent and compelling.

It should be organized in a way that is both informative and interesting. The compliant résumé has all of the sections that are required to show the prospective employer that you meet or exceed the requirements of the position.

Because most résumés are submitted electronically as an attachment to an e-mail or web site application, you need to ensure that the format you are using downloads to the receiver in a way that mirrors the hard copy version you have worked so hard to create. Always send résumés in pdf format to prevent printing errors by the person receiving your résumé.

Remember, the résumé is designed to get you to the next phase of the hiring process: the interview. It is not intended to present all of your qualifications – just what is needed to get you an interview. Focus on content and meeting the expectations of the hiring manager reviewing your résumé.

> "The purpose of the résumé is to get you an interview, not a job."

There have been thousands of books written on how to write a quality résumé. The reason there are so many is that there is no right way to write a résumé. Everyone has an opinion on what works. They propose how best to get the attention of the recruiter and the hiring manager, but if the résumé is not compliant, it will not get past the first screening filter of the hiring office.

There are lots of things *not* to include in your résumé. Never include a personal picture or personal data. The types of personal data that you should avoid are social security number, date of birth, marital status, children, references, or salary requirements.

Make Yourself Indispensable

On-Line Résumé Folder

Often times, it is the boring work that makes the difference long-term. In this case, I suggest that the foundation for making and maintaining a quality résumé is to regularly collect information in an on-line résumé data folder. In this folder, capture and include everything about your career, your jobs, your awards, letters of recommendation, education, transcripts, potential references, and special training.

> "The foundation for making and maintaining a quality résumé is to regularly collect information in an on-line résumé data folder."

The strategy behind the on-line résumé data folder is that you will have one place to access a complete record of your career-relevant facts.

Having all of this information in one place will help you to remember and accurately cite key information about your experience or training. In addition, as your career evolves and possibly your objectives change, you might dust off some awards or accomplishments you have not used in previous résumés. You may use these specifics to highlight a career theme that will be useful as you refine your résumé in the subsequent coherent and compelling phases.

For example, I recently was asked whether I had any experience in facilitation. Several years ago, I completed a three-day course to be certified as a facilitator but I never took the time to add the training to my résumé data folder. It took me hours to find my certificate of completion, the name of the organization providing the training, and the dates of the training. Had I taken the time, when I finished the training, to add it to my résumé data folder I could have saved lots of time and energy.

I now make it a practice to update my on-line résumé data folder monthly with this type of information. There is no better time to update your experience and your accomplishments than when the details are still fresh in your memory.

> "There is no better time to update your experience and your accomplishments than when you are doing the job."

One way to get started in building a complete résumé is to "storyboard" your career. I recommend that you take a blank sheet of paper and literally begin to draft your career history almost as if you are writing an autobiography. If you are a recent college graduate your storyboard will be shorter than someone who has been employed for 20 years but the process is the same.

Do not be concerned about format; focus on content and making sure you have covered your professional life in the most complete way possible. You might be surprised by experiences or training that you have had over the years that for whatever reason have not made it on your previous résumés. Be sure to include the positions between semesters in college, volunteer efforts, and anything that would demonstrate initiative and learning.

A common construct to use in a résumé is to state a *problem* that you tackled then a *solution* you produced to resolve the problem from which an organization gained a positive *result*. I call this the PSR framework.

> "Explain your work experiences within a problem, solution, and result (PSR) framework."

This strategy will pay dividends later in the interview process, as the interviewer will focus on this kind of information as a way of exploring how you have demonstrated your key competencies in previous positions.

Most résumés are history stories. They describe where the candidate has been and what he/she did for a specific period of time. As a result, the potential employer now has to take the information that the job seeker has supplied on the résumé and make a judgment as to whether or not the job seeker can be successful in the job they are attempting to fill. This transference cannot be assumed; you must make it easy for the person reading your résumé to project how you will perform in the future.

Make Yourself Indispensable

It is the ability to apply your current competencies to solve future problems that you must prove to the reader. This is optimally done in the PSR framework

> "It is the ability to apply your current competencies to solve future problems that you must prove to the reader."

Most résumés, once they get into the hands of the hiring manager or recruiter are reviewed quickly. A decision is made by the reviewer in a matter of seconds as to whether or not they will read beyond page one.

As a reviewer, if I open a résumé and page one is not "compliant" in terms of what I need or want in order to make an intelligent decision to say yes or no on your candidacy, the résumé is probably never even get to page two.

> "If page one of a résumé does not include both the essential basics and something to catch the reader's attention, they will probably never even look at page two."

The following are detailed descriptions of elements of a compliant résumé.

Header: The header includes your name and contact information (both mailing and e-mail addresses). Do not use humorous or inappropriate e-mail addresses. You can create one on Google or Yahoo for free so consider creating a new e-mail to use for all of

125

Make Yourself Indispensable

your job search activity. This makes it easy to track and find e-mail traffic related to your job search.

If you use your cell phone as your primary number then you need to be careful how you answer any call. A call from a prospective employer can come at any time, so when the phone rings during happy hour at the local pub and you answer the call, be ready to take the call professionally or just let it go to voice mail.

Career Objective: The career objective is often the first thing I review on a résumé. Draft a career objective that ties into the position you want and your career strategy. Do not include a statement that says something like "a job or assignment that makes the best use of my talent or experience." A statement like that says you have not done your homework. You obviously have little, if any, knowledge of the company to which you are applying and you have no vision for your own career progression.

The Career Objective is the section that will be refined during the coherent and compelling phases as you glean out your discriminating characteristics that make you a "have to see this person" candidate. Again, be memorable and honest. If you are not going after a specific job opening then the career objective provides insight into what would be your "ideal" job.

Qualifications Summary: If you are a more experienced candidate with credentials and qualifications that you believe are very well aligned to the vacancy announcement, you may decide to include a qualifications summary vice a career objective. I find that the more aligned they are to the position, the candidate is better served by using the critical space on page one with a well-written qualifications summary. The end result has to be written in a way that allows the reader to easily see that the candidate has the right credentials for the opportunity under consideration.

Key Skills: The qualifications summary would appear right after the header in place of or right after the career objective. However, if you do not include a qualifications summary, you should consider adding a list of your key skills. These define what you do, what makes you a really good candidate, what sets you apart from the competition, and what makes you a "must interview" candidate.

More importantly, as a recruiter, if I am reading hundreds of résumés in search of that core group of candidates that I want to interview, you will want to make sure that your key skills list makes it easy to tie you and your expertise to the vacancy announcement. Finding the key words all in one place makes my job easy. The more experience you have, the more likely that the list of key skills will move to the second page. It may not be real interesting but it will have the words needed for a key word search.

Providing clearly what you are really good at (e.g., "passionate writer" or "detail-oriented customer service skills") makes it easier for me to differentiate you from the other candidates' résumés and to put you on that "must interview" list.

Make Yourself Indispensable

<u>Work Experience</u>: Provide a chronological listing of jobs with the most recent first. This should constitute the majority of the chronological résumé and should concentrate on the last ten years of your professional experience. If you do not have ten years of experience then include all of your experience.

> "The work experience section on the first page of your résumé should cover your last ten years of experience."

However, those of you who find yourself in a job search at the middle or end of your career, the recruiter is going to be most interested in what you have done "recently" and how have you stayed on top of your profession. Just doing your assigned work is not good enough.

For example, have you stayed current on relevant technology? Are you active in professional associations, career-specific training, and professional conferences? It speaks volumes to the recruiter if you have stayed current in your field.

The most critical aspect of this section is to condense your work history into a series of problem-solution-result vignettes. These establish the value you brought to the organization and hints at your ability to be able to solve future problems.

<u>Education</u>: Find a way to get your "core" education on page one of the résumé if you have fewer than 5-10 years of experience. As an experienced hiring manager for both public and private

sector jobs, my review process of résumés leads me to three areas immediately: Career Objective, Key Skills, and Education.

Page one is a must for education early in your career but as you mature in the work environment, the work experience begins to take precedence over the formal high school, college, and graduate education. I want to know where you received the training and developed the skills thus far in your career.

When you list your education include name of the school, year graduated, degree received, and any "special" areas of study or concentration. I have noticed that résumé writers often leave out special training and even graduate work in a non-related field. I would recommend including that information but maybe not on page one. Only include grade point average (GPA) while you are still in school or have fewer than five years of experience after school.

At this point do not worry about length of the résumé. We will compress the résumé later as you move toward a compelling résumé.

Certifications, Professional Organizations, Clearances, etc.: Often there are separate sections for certifications, memberships in professional organizations, publications, patents, clearances, etc., depending upon your profession. Reference any specialized experience that can add to your case to be interviewed for the position or may differentiate you from other candidates.

These special "talents" can be critical to getting an interview. For example, if you are a program manager it is relevant that you

Make Yourself Indispensable

have completed your Project Management Professional (PMP) certification. This achievement should be clearly noted in your résumé. Include the PMP next to your name on the top of the résumé on page one and include the detail associated with how and when you earned the PMP on page two under professional certifications.

I have never been a big fan of listing awards on résumés. The awards are often company-specific so they are not really a professional credential. The performance that led to the award is what is important and needs to be reflected in your accomplishments under experience. If the award is industry-wide or international, then definitely include it.

Some companies use software to scan résumés to identify and select ones for review that include the key words identified as essential credentials to be considered as a viable candidate for hire. This might include technical training, a particular college or university, programming languages, fluency in foreign language, prior residence abroad, job titles, etc.

If a position requires that you have five years of experience in sales, make sure you actually say that in your résumé in a way that it will be picked up in a scan of the résumé by the software. Do not assume that the chronology of your experience will get you past the screening.

Résumés should highlight the same credentials that the job announcement highlights as the key skills or experience for competitive candidates.

Make Yourself Indispensable

Coherent and Compelling – Refining the Message

Now that your résumé is compliant and complete, you need to check for logical consistency between your career objective or the job being pursued and the rest of your résumé (i.e., coherency). You will remove information that does not help to convince a prospective employer of your value and enhance the resonance of your message (i.e., become compelling).

The end result of a compelling résumé is that you provide the essentials needed to get an interview and get the reader excited about meeting you! If you can change the name at the top of your résumé and have it represent your office mate with little trouble, you do not have a compelling résumé!

There must be a purpose for everything you include in your résumé. The coherency and compelling phase is really about content refinement.

> "There must be a purpose for everything you include in your résumé."

While it may be a little controversial, this might be a good place to include any figure or a visual to replace many paragraphs worth of information.

The use of "people verbs" at this point helps to make the impression that you actually do things. Adjectives such as exceptional, world-class, and extraordinary are only relevant if spoken about you by someone else. Explain accurately what you did and let the reviewer determine if it is "exceptional."

Make Yourself Indispensable

Coherency implies that the résumé facts are self-consistent within the résumé. For example, do specifics of your education reinforce your experience? Are two sections confusing because one focuses on highly technical skills and the other focuses on your leadership acumen?

During this phase, you look for duplication. It may be okay to leave in duplication, if you have it in there for impact. Conversely, eliminate duplication to refine the message; do not confuse, distract, or bore the reader. You also eliminate material that distracts from the core message you are trying to state with your résumé.

Just as a radio signal becomes clearer when background noise is eliminated, a résumé becomes more compelling as you eliminate any information that does not directly support the key messages of your résumé.

For your work experience, your education, and your qualifications summary sections figure out a one-word summary for each. Jot these words in the left margin then look at them together.

For example, for Darren's résumé (provided as an example in the appendix) the summary words might have read: write, negotiate, crafty, physics, space, research, innovation, and energy.

Are your summary words similar or are they a vision of contrast? Use the message you glean from this exercise as you transition into the compelling stage. Darren's summary words hint at the diversity of topics he enjoys (and differentiates him from others) yet still is grounded in science and technology.

> "For each section of your résumé, jot down a one-word summary – do they collectively tell a story consistent with your career objective or the job you are pursuing?"

How long do professional recruiters look at your résumé? Seven minutes? Five minutes? Two minutes? Actually, just six seconds. So, you had best not provide a résumé that sounds like every other résumé they have seen. But, how do you stand out?

Again, the résumé should not exceed two pages.[12] However, if you have a special skill that you have continually developed over the last 20 years that is a key element of the position announcement, you will want to adopt a résumé format that allows you to highlight that special skill in greater detail on page one of your résumé.

---

[12] The only exception to the two-page rule is the resume in pursuit of a federal job, here size does matter. The federal government is a unique employer. They have position descriptions that are many pages in length, some for example are twenty pages long. And because they are long with many "must have or required qualifications." The resume you submit must be all inclusive of your skills and competencies and with lots of detail. If you miss one requirement in your resume, you do not make the list as a candidate. The down-selected subset of applicants is referred to as the cert list. All the recommendations presented on improving your resume still apply.

Make Yourself Indispensable

What makes your résumé compelling is how you describe your experience and qualifications summary while eliminating anything that does not support that focus.

I have been a recruiter in the federal government and a hiring manager for private sector employers. Most résumés tell me nothing about what you have accomplished in the jobs you have held in the past or the likelihood that you will be successful in my position in the future. Can you solve problems, create solutions, provide outstanding customer service, and be the new team leader in sales? Your compelling résumé has to answer the mail on the ability to solve future problems and do it efficiently.

> "Your compelling résumé must concisely show your ability to solve *future* problems."

I cannot overemphasize the need for all résumés to be full of PSR vignettes, these produce the "so what factor." For example, as a real estate agent you turned around a money-losing office by landing annual sales in excess of $10M for the past five years leading to the company going public. This is an excellent storyline!

Similarly, if you were an administrative assistant for the President of Company XYZ and you realigned the work processes of the internal administrative team resulting in a cost savings of $300k. This is a solid PSR vignette.

Think about how you have influenced the way that work in your current job is getting done today vice before you arrived. This is the best way to begin to identify your "so what" factors, often in the format of problem-solution-result.

I have many clients who complain that their work in a particular job did not lend itself to the strategy of "how did I make the position or company better." They believe that only people who work in sales or who work in a job that has lots of metrics are able to measure the impact they have had in a particular assignment.

However, I have yet to find a client that was not able to provide examples of how they made a difference in each position they held in their career, if they thought long and hard.

Take the time to think about your assignments and how you made a difference. The same information (especially the PSR vignettes) can often be used in the interview when you discuss your success. Building a compelling résumé makes the interview easier.

> "A compelling résumé not only gets you an interview, it makes the interview easier."

Another key element of a compelling résumé is the clarity of how you acquired and positioned your key skills. How are they demonstrated in your job performance over the last couple of assignments?

If a key requirement of the position being pursued is outstanding customer service, what evidence can you provide that you have strong customer service skills and have demonstrated those skills in your previous positions? Where is the evidence? If you have been making entries regularly into your on-line resume data folder it will be easier to unearth this evidence.

Make sure you take the time to consider the job announcement and how you can best demonstrate on paper how you are the best candidate to interview for the position. If your résumé is not compelling enough to get you past the recruiter and into an interview with the hiring manager, it does not matter how qualified you are for the job. A compelling résumé coupled with a great network is the formula for career success.

> "A compelling résumé coupled with a great network is the formula for career success."

Your résumé should be an accurate reflection of you – both your profession and your personality. I recommend that once you have drafted what you believe is a compelling two-page résumé, share it with someone who knows you and ask the question, "Does this résumé speak to who I am and what I have accomplished in my career to date?" Often, the reviewer will say yes but also might identify something that they know that is significant in your background that you have overlooked or given too little emphasis.

Do not underestimate the power of being remembered, liked, and respected. Facts are easy to forget; feelings are difficult to get out of your head. This also holds for the recruiter and hiring manager.

> "The résumé should reflect both your profession and your personality."

Make Yourself Indispensable

When I am coaching clients through the career transition process and we review their accomplishments for the résumé, they often suggest omitting accomplishments that were from being part of a team. They do not feel it fair to take credit for the work or the team's performance. You can explain that you were part of a team that was successful in accomplishing something special. Noting this on the résumé does two things. It provides the reader information on what you accomplished and that you can work effectively as a member of a team.

Do you think a player for a professional sports team that wins a world championship does not include the accomplishment on their résumé because they were "just a member of the team?" I suspect that Derek Jeter's résumé includes references to the New York Yankees' five world championships during his career.

A résumé that "sings" is one that tells the reader of your successes, like "increased sales by 100%." Just telling me you increased sales, however, is not enough. How did you increase sales by 100% and what was the situation that required your action? For example, "through the development of marketing algorithms to combat a poorly performing marketing team, sales revenue doubled - the best performance of the last ten years." A statement that shows problem, solution, and result gets my attention!

Brag a little with facts and verbs, not adjectives! Get my attention and make me want to see how your skills apply to my job opening. Remember, the purpose of the résumé is to get an interview, not a job. The interview is the next step. Do not try to do it all in one step.

Make Yourself Indispensable

"The purpose of the résumé is to get an interview, not a job. Do not try to do both in one step."

A good exercise at this point is to describe what you do and who you are in seven words! Examine your summary words from the last phase but use verbs (rather than adjectives) whenever possible. This may be tough for you to do but you must try.

We are looking here for the hallelujah moment when someone reads the résumé and says, "I have to meet this person!" You want your personality and traits that single you out of the huddled masses to come out in your résumé at this point. If you say that you are a friendly, jovial person, then use friendly, jovial words. If you say that you communicate well, include figures and diagrams to reinforce that.

The figure below shows an example of where one can basically teach a graduate level course in organizational productivity with ten terms with seven words each. The ten terms are grouped into three convenient categories; this grouping helps the reader to understand the scope of the topic organizational productivity.

Each individual component's seven-word brand focuses on substantive words: verbs (i.e., action), nouns (i.e., what), and impactful (not flowery) adjectives. As you can see, it is possible to create a compelling message with seven carefully selected words.

Organizational Productivity:
Ten Terms with Seven Words Each

Knowledge - retains and recalls useful information and processes
Maturity - responds responsibly to the actions of others   **} INDIVIDUAL**
Wisdom - avoids cognitive biases to make good decisions

Management - directs diverse people, projects, and programs effectively
Leadership - decisively inspires others to attain group goals   **} TEAM**
Creativity - generates and communicates new ideas and concepts
Innovation - derives value from implementation of creative solutions

Strategy - plan of attack to achieve shared vision
Productivity - performs and leverages tasks and projects efficiently   **} ORGANIZATION**
Sustainability - executes with persistent, reliable, and consistent productivity

Darren's seven word brand from his résumé in the appendix is *"creating multi-disciplinary solutions to empower enduring productivity."*

Once you have your mantra make sure that every word in your résumé supports your "brand" (i.e., your seven-word summary). This seven-word summary may even become your career objective.

You can equate reading a compelling résumé to listening to a song that causes you to tap the beat of the song on the table continuously. In other words, is there some hook in your résumé that people walk away remembering easily?

At this point, do not be afraid of "white space": having more words does not necessarily mean your résumé is more compelling. You have seen the people who are so impressed with themselves that they have to fill the paper completely with six point font; there is no white space. You must guard against that and create white space to invite people to come and read the words and not be overwhelmed by them. Overwhelm the reader with clarity, not content.

> "For your résumé, overwhelm the reader with clarity, not content."

The compelling component of writing a résumé is very much like branding a product. You need to differentiate yourself from others that the hiring manager may be considering.

Do not say you are a "great systems engineer" because there are millions of system engineers on the market today. However, if you say you are a "systems engineer who leverages medical imaging techniques to solve intelligence problems," you have differentiated yourself from the pack.

Clearly, however, you need to be careful in differentiation that you don't put yourself into such a narrow marketplace that very few people would see your utility or have a position for you.

Again, the compelling part must include clear communication, especially the resonance. For example, use "before" versus "after" or "with" versus "without" to contrast. The rhythm to the résumé will make it very powerful, much like Martin Luther King's "I Have a Dream" speech that focused on what "was" versus what "could be."

Make Yourself Indispensable

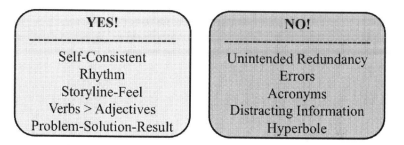

RESUME RULES

YES!	NO!
Self-Consistent	Unintended Redundancy
Rhythm	Errors
Storyline-Feel	Acronyms
Verbs > Adjectives	Distracting Information
Problem-Solution-Result	Hyperbole

Exude passion and excitement. If you are not enthused about your accomplishments why would you expect total strangers to be motivated to meet you just by reading your résumé?

Remember, text only contains 10% of the message (the other 90% is in body language and tone of voice) so it must be compelling if they cannot hear and see you deliver your value proposition.

How do people feel after reading your résumé? You can send a powerfully clear message without bragging. You can be passionate without lacking technical competence!

It has to be compelling – it has to give the reader that something special that makes the reader wanting to know more and hopefully issue an invite for a personal conversation or interview.

There is no excuse for not having a résumé ready to share with a recruiter or hiring official, if requested.

Make Yourself Indispensable

The Fifth "C" – Correct!

Everything you put on a résumé has to be true. Making false statements on a résumé can lead to termination after getting the job.

There was a case in my area where a school administrator falsified his academic accomplishments, stating on his résumé that he had both an undergraduate degree and a graduate degree in education.

Unfortunately, he had neither. He had been teaching in a local school district, but the prior school administration did not do a reference check on his earlier application. It was only after he applied for a more senior position that his false entries got noticed.

Therefore, the final rule for a compelling résumé is probably a rule you have heard before: be honest!

The résumé that you plan to share with recruiters, staffing managers, hiring managers, headhunters, and to launch your LinkedIn profile must be immaculate! It must be accurate and kept up to date at all times.

There is no excuse for sending out a résumé that has typographical, spelling, or punctuation errors – no exceptions!

Read your résumé regularly, run it through spell and grammar check, have a trusted friend read and re-read the résumé to make sure it is error-free. Your résumé is a reflection of you!

Make Yourself Indispensable

Sample Résumés

There are a couple of examples of compelling résumés in the appendix for you to see how you might condense and tailor your résumé.

One is for an individual with over 30 years of experience (my coauthor Darren McKnight) and a college senior, who landed a great internship with her compelling resume this year.

Remember that you need to think about a résumé as a marketing slick of *and* for you! Do not be forgotten: use figures and "people verbs." Be specific and do not speak in hyperbole. Do use problem - solution - result as a framework for describing your activities; show wisdom and exude passion. Prior success is important but a proven capability to be a success again is what employers are looking for.

Elevator Speech

One of the most important pieces of the job search process is creating an elevator speech. The elevator speech is basically a summary of who you are and why you are someone that people would like in their network.

It is a concise, compelling summary of "who you are." It should be as natural and as easy as saying your name. Your seven-word brand may be a great starting point for your elevator speech.

The elevator speech is important to have even when you are not in a job search. When you are at a business gathering, social

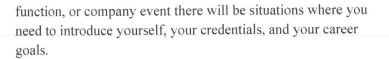

function, or company event there will be situations where you need to introduce yourself, your credentials, and your career goals.

You should have something ready to say. At a minimum, you should have your seven-word brand generated for your résumé at the ready.

Not being prepared to take advantage of a chance encounter to impress a potential networking partner or future employer reflects poorly on you and in a job search process.

The following boxed text is a long elevator speech for a job seeker.

> "Hello, my name is John Smith. I am a graduate of Loyola University where I earned a degree in Communications. I have experience with many kinds of communication systems and media formats. I am most interested in opportunities that would allow me to deploy the latest wideband solutions to a mobile workforce. I am currently employed outside my industry and would be interested in talking with any company where my credentials may be of value. I am open to relocation and when not working I enjoy coaching local youth basketball and volunteering at my church."

You need a "hook"; it should be something that the listener will remember. Make it results- and action-oriented but, but most important, it needs to be interesting and memorable.

You should take a hard look at the position and align three to five things from your credentials that match very well with the position in question. You should fold some of those into your elevator speech. When you are being interviewed and the hiring manager says "tell me about yourself," you should be ready with your elevator speech.

> "Your elevator speech, PSR vignettes, and seven-word brand are all useful for the interview process."

For example, a position may require a special credential such as PMP, so you could say:

> "Thank you again for the opportunity to interview for this lead analyst position. I am interested in a position that leverages my strengths so I can make the maximum impact on the organization. I recently completed my PMP certification with XYZ School and have enjoyed working as a program manager for the last three years. Now, with the PMP certification, I am even more prepared to make a valuable contribution to your firm. I enjoy travel and working with new clients."

With this opening statement, you have covered several issues. First, you showed your interest in the opportunity. Second, you explained that you have completed your PMP and received the PMP from a recognized training or academic institution. Third, you have provided your years of experience. Fourth, you highlighted that you are open to and interested in travel, as required by the position. Last, you detailed how you like talking to and meeting new clients.

Make Yourself Indispensable

You have answered some of the questions for the hiring manager right up front and have not had to look for an opportunity on your own to promote how you and your credentials match the job.

Now you can settle into a conversation about the company, the work environment, and how it will fit with your interests. Instead of dreading the "tell me about yourself" question, use it to your advantage.

Do not come to the interview without researching and rehearsing. If you just "wing it" for the interview why should the hiring manager expect that you will come to work prepared?

> "Do not come to the interview without researching and rehearsing."

The Bio-Profile

One additional way to present your credentials is the professional biographic profile (i.e., bio-profile). The bio-profile is a one-page document that tells your story in one page.

I know, you are already mad at me for telling you that you have to keep your résumé to two pages plus creating PSR vignettes, a seven-word brand, and an elevator speech.

Now, I'm telling you to collect your credentials in a different format. Let me explain. A bio-profile includes a small picture, contact information, and enough information about you that even your closest friend would say "I didn't know that about you."

The bio-profile is longer than your elevator speech but shorter than your résumé.

The format is simple. It is basically a three-paragraph document that introduces you to the reader. It really does serve as an informal introduction to you as a person, not just a candidate.

Paragraph one is a long version of your elevator speech with details about your experience; depth and diversity of credentials; and what you are currently doing. The first paragraph of my human capital bio-profile is:

> "Roger Campbell has 40 years of experience in both the public and private sector as a human capital expert, executive coach, and management consultant. He has led major change initiatives in recruitment, talent management, workforce planning, employer branding, and workforce analysis. Roger is currently serving as an executive coach in the Intelligence Community and in support of several civilian agencies in the federal government."

In a matter of about 10 seconds everyone reading my bio-profile has a sense of who I am and what I am currently doing in my career field.

Make Yourself Indispensable

The second paragraph explains my experience in more depth. It might be more useful to have several different bio-profiles ready if you are active in multiple industries.

I take 40 years of human capital experience and I condense it into one paragraph and focus the reader's attention to what I consider to be my industry "headlines."

The second paragraph does not include dates of employment or when I did the work; it is more about the work itself.

The second paragraph of my bio-profile is:

"Mr. Campbell is the former Chief Human Capital Officer for the National Reconnaissance Office and is a former senior human capital manager with the Central Intelligence Agency (CIA). After a successful career at CIA, he served as the Director of Consulting Services for Monster Government Solutions, a division of Monster.com. He has worked as a senior consultant and advisor for some of the most respected management consulting companies in the country. Roger has published articles and has led webcasts on topics associated with human capital challenges in both the public and private sectors. He continues to develop precision hiring strategies to help organizations hire the right talent."

The third, and last, paragraph is all about education and training. It includes where one went to school, degrees, certifications, and any special training that supports what you have outlined in paragraph two.

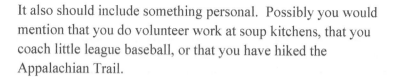
It also should include something personal. Possibly you would mention that you do volunteer work at soup kitchens, that you coach little league baseball, or that you have hiked the Appalachian Trail.

The third paragraph of my bio-profile is:

> "Roger is a graduate of George Mason University (GMU) and has completed graduate work at both GMU and American University. He is certified by the International Coaching Federation as an executive coach and is a graduate of the Georgetown University (GU) Program for Executive Coaching. He serves on the advisory board for the Center For Human Capital Innovation and the National Security Association Worldwide (NSAWW). Roger volunteers his services as a coach and mentor to senior executives in the public sector and serves as a guest lecturer on human capital related topics at the CIA, GMU, and GU. He resides in Northern Virginia with Candi, his wife of 39 years, and is the proud father of four successful consultants."

Include a small picture and accurate contact information on the top of the bio-profile. The photograph should be professional – not something that you took on your camping trip or last vacation with friends. There are plenty of vendors who will take your photograph with a professional backdrop and will give you the results almost immediately after taking the pictures. There is no excuse for not having a quality photograph available when needed for your bio-profile or any event where a photograph is needed.

Why do you need a bio-profile and why create multiple versions? If you meet a friend at a social event and the conversation leads to a discussion about careers and the person you are talking with suggests that your credentials would be a nice fit for his company, you want to have information on hand to follow-up immediately.

If there is a potential opportunity then send your résumé and bio-profile to your friend. The bio-profile acts as an ice-breaker while the résumé provides the relevant content. Instead of your friend trying to introduce you using only your résumé, the bio-profile efficiently introduces you to the potential hiring manager.

The résumé is there to seal the deal but with the bio-profile you suddenly go from being just another résumé to someone who appears "human," not just another piece of paper. You have basically personalized the process and moved the conversation to the next level without even being there.

I have prepared two versions of my bio-profile: one for my human capital experience and one based on my executive coaching experience. Trust me, I have found multiple uses for a quality bio-profile and you will to. The executive coaching bio-profile is in the appendix.

Where to Send a Résumé

Make Yourself Indispensable

Now that you have a compelling résumé, what do you do with it?
With the advent of the internet, the number of people who can
see your résumé in a short time has made many people lazy
about writing a résumé.

Networking is more than just putting together a list of people
you need to notify or alert that you are in the job market. You
have to have an enduring plan on how to make that list come
alive and work for you in your job search. This means keeping
your network alive even when you are not looking for a job.

There are millions of people on the internet, but that doesn't
mean that anybody is going to read your résumé. There are
important issues about the résumé in the 21st century
information technology era.

I provide a monthly briefing to soon-to-be transitioning federal
employees of various salary and experience levels. I suggest to
this group of very astute and experienced professionals that once
they create a compelling résumé that they should have it with
them at all times.

I have heard of individuals who passed along their résumés at
church gatherings, on the sidelines at a soccer match, or in line at
a grocery store.

> "When looking for a new job, always have a
> hard copy of your résumé with you."

Giving someone a hard copy of your résumé often results in the
résumé being hand-carried to the hiring manager or recruiter
with a comment about how you are someone who should be
invited in for an interview. You have just gone from the bottom

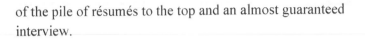

of the pile of résumés to the top and an almost guaranteed interview.

What does this mean for you? For you introverts who avoid events or activities where you have to meet new people, this is really hard work. To talk about yourself, promote your accomplishments, describe your education, and explain your credentials can be extremely uncomfortable.

Even handing someone a résumé can be stressful; get over it! It is your future you are talking about, do not shortchange yourself by waiting to be asked for your résumé. The worst thing they can do is recycle it.

Extroverts, on the other hand, usually don't have a problem marketing themselves. However, it really does not matter whether you are an introvert or an extrovert: if your collateral material (i.e., résumé, elevator speech, etc.) is not ready, you will miss opportunities.

> "If your collateral material (i.e., résumé, elevator speech, etc.) is not ready, you will miss opportunities."

As mentioned earlier, automated tools can do a keyword search of your résumé, based on the key qualifications and competencies that have been highlighted as important in the job announcement. If you do not include these key words in your résumé, you run the risk of being overlooked in the review process.

Make Yourself Indispensable

It is important to be "compliant" with your career field by using the correct terminology, especially early in your career. However, the keyword search capability still is only used to decide which résumés should be given further consideration; it does not get you a job. It only prevents you from getting an interview.

Job Boards

Even though most job openings are filled through networking, you cannot ignore the reach that job boards can provide for your compelling résumé to be seen by others.

Jobs are often listed on an organization's web site but you must be smart enough and conscientious enough to regularly look at the web site of an organization for which you want to work. You must also react quickly enough to the vacancy announcement to get an opportunity to compete for that job. If it is a friend, mentor, coach, or family member who alerts you to an internal job posting, you might get a jump on your competition.

There are a number of web sites where you can submit your résumé to be considered by potential employers and recruiters. Everybody has their favorites but we will review four that have been highly successful for job placement: Monster, Indeed, LinkedIn, and USAJOBS.

> "Four key job boards to monitor are Monster, Indeed, LinkedIn, and USAJOBS."

Make Yourself Indispensable

The biggest value in job boards and company web sites is that they announce career opportunities. However, they are also useful sources of information. They include details about the company and the job that will help you make a decision about whether or not you want to pursue that position and also prepare you better for the potential interview.

The position announcements on job boards contain critical real-time information about openings and the qualifications that the hiring organization has decided it needs in a viable candidate. Use this information to tailor your résumé. You can add opportunity-specific words and phrases that will make your résumé more likely to generate an interview.

When I hear candidates complain that it is hard to find information about positions or companies advertising vacancies, it usually means they have not tried very hard to find information.

I remember as a recruiter for the federal government in the 1980's that it was difficult to find candidates. We used the media available at the time and the most cost-effective medium was the newspaper. Most readers from that era will remember how the classified section of the local newspaper was the place to look for a job. If you wanted a job in another city you had to find a way to secure a copy of their newspaper to see who was hiring there and how to apply.

Today, the web allows for advertising a job 24/7, worldwide, and for as long as you care to pay to have the advertisement on the internet. The internet and job boards have changed how candidates look for work and how companies advertise their jobs. Mining a résumé database linked to a job board allows employers to find passive job candidates, candidates who are in the job market, candidates open to calls from recruiters, or those who may not have seen the job announcement that you want to bring to their attention.

-Monster.com – The First Job Board

Jeff Taylor launched Monster as a "job board" in 1994. His company, Adion, was acquired by TMP (Telephone Marketing Programs, a Yellow Pages Company) and Jeff was named CEO. In 1995, Monster began marketing its services and was immediately picked up in 48 countries and averaged 15,000 visitors a day to its web site.

In 2006, Monster.com bought advertising space during the Super Bowl. The cost of an advertisement during the Super Bowl telecast was about a million dollars for 30 seconds and Monster.com launched a great advertisement about what a young girl wanted to be when she grew up. The ad cost a ton of money and you know who paid for the ad – companies buying job announcements on Monster.com.

In 2010, it was still promoting an average of 63 million job seekers per month. Today, Monster continues to be the brand associated with job boards and on-line hiring. However, there have been thousands of other companies that have joined the market of on-line hiring.

Make Yourself Indispensable

Monster.com is still the most recognized job board in the world and provides a way for employers to advertise for jobs across the world instead of only in their hometowns. It is estimated that Monster.com now has over a million job postings and well over a million résumés in its database.

-Indeed.com

A fast rising on-line hiring resource is a company called Indeed.com. Indeed has been around since 2004 and it has slowly become the most visited job site in the United States. As of March 2014, it serviced 140 million visitors every month. Indeed is a great source for jobs because it actually feeds off the other job boards for its data. It is kept up to date and is available in 50 countries and 28 languages.

As a recruiter and as a job seeker, it is my number one source for up to date information about jobs around the world. If I am working with a transition client in Washington, D.C. who wants to know about jobs in Seattle, one click on Indeed.com can produce any and all jobs being advertised in the Seattle area.

-LinkedIn

The newcomer to the employment dance is LinkedIn. LinkedIn is a useful resource for both recruiters and job seekers. I talk with lots of recruiters and hiring managers today and many of them tell me that LinkedIn has become their number one source for candidates. LinkedIn was started in 2002 as a social networking service, a way for professionals to update business associations and their résumé on the web.

Make Yourself Indispensable

LinkedIn now has over 300 million members in 200 countries and is available in 20 languages. LinkedIn membership grows by two members every second. The basic membership is free and if you want to be seen and heard as a potential hire for any company in any industry, you need to have a professional profile on LinkedIn.

> "LinkedIn now has over 300 million members and it grows by two members every second."

Using the information available to you on the internet can often give you great information on positions and opportunities and also on the key players in the company. The more you know about the company, its programs, needs, and leadership the better prepared you will be to develop a résumé that is going to get their attention and that interview you seek.

Darren and I are both on LinkedIn; we are looking forward to connecting with you.

-USAJOBS.GOV

The federal government decided to move into the 21st century recruiting world when it launched USAJOBS.GOV in 2003. It is the federal government's way of advertising job openings for most federal departments and agencies in one place. Few people know that when the Office of Personnel Management (OPM) decided to build a centralized job board, they hired Monster.com to design, develop, and manage it.

Make Yourself Indispensable

Monster ran the job board for nearly eight years before OPM decided they could save money by doing it themselves. Monster, through their management of USAJOBS, encouraged federal agencies to shorten the job announcements from thirty to five pages, to rewrite their announcements to make them more appealing to the public, and to promote a more efficient application process. It continues to evolve and improve.

Applicants can load up to five résumés on the job site and receive automated announcements when jobs that fit their profile become active on USAJOBS.

One thing that USAJOBS does not allow is for federal agencies to "mine" the huge database of résumés OPM has secured since the job board was created in 2003. OPM is sitting on hundreds of thousands of résumés and they do not allow any agency to search the résumé database for candidates. They could probably find candidates for most of their vacancies if they did allow these searches, but according to OPM doing so would violate the spirit of open competition for jobs.

If you are a job seeker, I encourage you to regularly check USAJOBS for opportunities. It is no secret that federal service provides competitive salaries and benefits plus above average opportunities for training, career development, and worldwide travel.

The application process for federal jobs may be harder and more time-consuming but the jobs can be exciting. It is also no secret that most federal agencies have an aging workforce with many vacancies today (and for years to come). There has never been a better time to look for a job in the federal government.

> "There has never been a better time to look for a job in the federal government."

On the 23rd of December 2014, I typed in the word "security" into the USAJOBS.GOV web site and 5,000 jobs were identified as available and in need of a candidate. So, stay alert to opportunities in the federal sector.

Company Web Sites

Even with Monster, Indeed, LinkedIn, and USAJOBS, you do not want to overlook the career centers of the companies in your target industry. Most companies advertise on their own web sites for candidates and those same jobs are not always found on the job boards. The cost associated with advertising jobs on any job board is an expense that many companies prefer to avoid.

If you are actively looking at what companies in your industry are doing in the hiring arena, keep close watch on their web sites. By close watch, I am suggesting that you visit the web site every day.

New jobs may be added to the web site on a daily basis and being the first to submit your résumé for a position is a great way to get the attention of the inside recruiters.

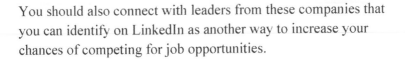

You should also connect with leaders from these companies that you can identify on LinkedIn as another way to increase your chances of competing for job opportunities.

Recruiters

If you cannot get a job through networking with your colleagues or through job board listings then you may try a recruiter. Actually, recruiters should be part of your established network and it is prudent to know several recruiters - plural! I have several good friends who are recruiters.

Most do specialize in a specific industry so you need to look carefully at a recruiter's pedigree to insure that it is consistent with your needs.

You will find that some recruiters have a worldwide coverage but most have a regional scope so you really need to get to know ones active in the geographic regions where you are interested in living.

It is likely that a recruiter will not have a ideal job right when you really need one, be patient. Recruiters are an important part of finding opportunities in the future. Incidentally, you should never have to pay one to do this job placement.

> "Recruiters are an important part of finding opportunities in the future but do not expect instant success."

In addition, good recruiters can provide you valuable feedback on your résumé and insightful intelligence on the overall job

160

Make Yourself Indispensable

market. Your time investment to engage in regular meetings with a few trusted recruiters will be worth it long-term.

Through networking, job boards, and recruiters your compelling résumé will likely get you one or more interviews. Let's now examine the art of winning the interview.

Winning the Interview

The interview process for the job actually starts with the first call you get from the hiring organization. Just because the person on the other end of the call is not the hiring manager, do not assume that the call or conversation is not important. That person on the other end of the call may have some influence on what candidates are recommended to be invited for an interview.

> "The interview process for the job actually starts with the first call you get from the hiring organization."

I would often give my administrative assistant ten résumés with a list of questions and instructed him or her to call all the candidates with the goal of getting as much information as possible in the call. I also asked for a recommendation as to which candidate was the most impressive on the call (i.e., who was pleasant, who was forthcoming with the information, and knowledgeable about the company).

I also asked whom they would recommend for me to interview. That first call could be the first line of the screening process, one of the many hurdles you need to clear in the hiring process.

Make Yourself Indispensable

Nothing is scarier than going to an interview at a company where you know no one. That is why I suggested earlier that you invest in helping and learning about other people. It is not just ten times better to meet with ten people. It is 10 x 10 = 100 times better because each of them is also likely to talk to ten or so people each. Do not expect something from these folks. Just listen, learn, and write things down. Does that sound familiar? You may find out about a job or an employer might find out about you.

While you need to be looking at jobs as ways to advance your career, there are some attributes of jobs that are likely to be consistent with career advancement. Here are three general issues to address when accepting an interview or selecting a new job that are often neglected.

1. <u>Pick a boss, not a job</u>. A great job on paper can be horrible in reality if your direct supervisor is poor quality or just rubs you the wrong way. Make sure you know who will be your boss plus their personal and professional priorities.

    Will your boss support you when you make mistakes and recognize you when you do well? Is your future boss happy? If not, you probably will not be happy either.

2. <u>No Lateral Moves</u>. Do not take a job that is basically your same job for a different organization. This does not help challenge you or advance your career. Just as important, this will come across as a personal insult to the people you are leaving and the gaining organization will likely see you as having plateaued professionally. As we said before; "If you

are not moving forward, you are moving backward."

3. <u>Scale with Quality, Not Quantity</u>. Select a position where the quality of your work is more important than the number of hours you work, deals you close, or leads you generate. The treadmill of numbers equating to success will eat up all of your time and energy.

   Clearly, performance is about objective results but be sure that your job includes building the foundation that drives the numbers rather than just the numbers themselves. An exception to this rule is a sales job. Sales jobs are almost always about quantity and number of transactions so compensation is largely tied to money brought in.

If your résumé is out "on the street" for consideration and you get a call from a résumé screener but you are in the middle of something, do not engage in a conversation. Do not take the call unless you are in a position to respond professionally to the questions the screener is asking.

If the call comes and you are not in a position to take the call, ask that you receive a return call at a time that is more convenient or just let it go to voice mail. Try to schedule the call that day so as not to delay the process, but you are not being fair to yourself if you accept the call and are not prepared to perform at your best.

Make Yourself Indispensable

The Interview

Once you have finally made it to an interview, there are a few simple rules to follow to maximize your probability of success (i.e., getting a job offer).

In discussing new job opportunities, be true to yourself. Do not say what you think interviewers want to hear. Say what you really believe. Too many people say that they want to work long hours and put the company first. They then act surprised when they are placed in jobs that require exactly that.

However, other folks have balanced, healthy lives because they said that that was important to them. What a shock! Sometimes, you get exactly what you ask for.

> "In an interview, be true to yourself; do not say what you think they want to hear."

During one interview, Darren told his future boss that he wanted to work out of the home one day a week to focus on deep, technically rich thoughts that would not occur in a day full of 30-minute meetings. The boss thought it was a great idea and Darren found out later that his boss had been quietly doing the same thing for years and he had recently been promoted to the corporate board of directors.

You also might find out whether your potential future boss is a workaholic who just wants a partner in the "salt mines." Interview your prospective bosses – how they like their jobs will have a large impact on how much you will enjoy yours.

Make Yourself Indispensable

The key to an interview is to get the interviewer(s) to talk more than you do. Be memorable in your conciseness, the use of "people verbs," and the absence of adjectives. People will notice!

In addition, if your interviewer is talking more than you, then you are learning more about the company and the people in it. This information will help you to make the best decision for your future.

> "The key to an interview is to get the interviewer(s) to talk more than you do."

Anticipate what questions you might be asked in the interview and practice your answers. Be prepared on all fronts. First, make sure you are well-schooled on the company that has taken the time to invite you in for a conversation.

Notice, I used the word "conversation" and not interview. When you think about it, the interview should be a conversation.

Now, let's think back to your compelling résumé. The segmenting of your work experience into short vignettes that follow a problem-solution-result format actually ends up being a powerful tool for your interviews.

You need to be concise and compelling in your answers – what better way to explain your positive qualities than the crafted parables that you used to describe your work experience.

Make Yourself Indispensable

> "What better way to explain your positive qualities during an interview than the PSR vignettes that you used to describe your work experience."

The interesting thing about your short PSR summaries of work accomplishments is that they are almost more interesting and compelling when you describe them as problem-solution-result. In this way, you contrast the before (problem) and after (result) and get the listener hooked wondering just how did you get those good results (i.e., your solution).

What happens next is a *conversation* about who you are, why you are interested in this opportunity, how you got to where you are today, how you picked your career track, and what positions have been most challenging.

Do not forget to bring pen and paper to the interview. As we discussed earlier, the interview is about learning and about showing your prospective employer that you "listen, learn, and write things down" as a rule. This shows respect for the interviewers and also helps you in retaining specific facts provided during the interview process.

It is amazing how stressful an interview can be and you will be happy to see that sheet of paper full of notes once your heart rate gets back to normal so that you can review what you learned about the job and maybe even about your interview performance.

Make Yourself Indispensable

One of the first questions you will usually get in the interview is either 1) "Tell me about yourself" or 2) "What do you know about XYZ Company." When you explain about yourself, be concise and relevant; do not ramble on for ten minutes.

You don't need to know the complete history of the company but you should have some knowledge of the company, how it makes money or serves society, and why you think it might be where you want to spend your next twenty years. Be prepared for these questions and practice your answers (i.e., research and rehearse).

Think about it. If someone were to ask you why you are a good employee or would be a great hire for any company, what would you say? What are your best qualities? How are they relevant to the job for which you are interviewing? How do you know they are outstanding qualities or key differentiators for you and only you? This is what you need to have ready when questions of this nature are presented in the interview.

However, be in control. Do not go on and on about how great you are. Explain the essential facts about you relative to the open position. After that, be inquisitive about the company and its culture.

In other words, it is important to be interesting but it is more important to be interested (in the job, the interviewers, and the company).

> "During an interview, it is important for you to be interesting but it is more important for you to be interested."

Make Yourself Indispensable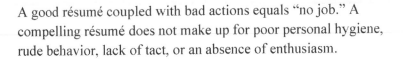

A good résumé coupled with bad actions equals "no job." A compelling résumé does not make up for poor personal hygiene, rude behavior, lack of tact, or an absence of enthusiasm.

During an interview, there are really only two kinds of questions they can ask: what and what-if. "What" questions deal with facts about yourself, your profession, or the job you are seeking. You need to come prepared having done your research on all of these aspects. If you do not know the answer, just say so; do not try to fake it.

"What-if" questions are behavioral in nature, asking how you would respond to a given situation. Again, leveraging the PSRs from your résumé is great practice for this challenge as you get more conversant at describing any situation in a logical structure of problem-solution-result.

The more that an interviewing organization promises, the less you should believe them. If an organization is telling you that you will be hired in as a director but within three years you could be a vice president, just ignore the vice president promise.

You have a bargaining position when you are hired. After that there is no motivation to give you anything that you do not earn. So, the more you are promised, the more you know that they are trying too hard to entice you.

> "The more they promise, the less you believe."

If they say you will be a director and explain that your performance will determine your future in the organization, go

168

Make Yourself Indispensable

with them. They are being honest and not trying to promise you things that they cannot guarantee. If you get a position, whether you keep it for 30 years or for three months is up to you and your immediate supervisor, and that's usually about it.

With that being said, conversely never say "no" to an interview, even if you know the opportunity is not a good fit. Take the interview: be positive, intelligent, and inquisitive. If you really are not a good fit there then they may try to find a better place or position. You might even impress them enough for them to create a job for you.

> "Never say "no" to an interview."

This is exactly what happened to Darren at SAIC. He interviewed for a job that he was not totally sure he was interested in accepting but when they were just getting ready to offer him the first job they asked what he wanted to be doing five years from now.

Darren explained his operational concept for a Chief Technology Officer (i.e., "engaged advocate for the technical workforce") and they said they needed that right now and created a new position just for him.

Follow-Up Actions

Never leave an interview without knowing what is going to happen next. I have been working in the talent management field for many years. I have coached hundreds of job seekers through the hiring process.

Make Yourself Indispensable

About ten years ago, when I transitioned out of government service into the private sector, I began a serious job search. I can remember going out to my first transition interview.

The night before the interview, I told my wife that I was ready and when I returned home from the interview she asked how the interview went. She asked simple questions such as did I like the job, did I like the people, and what is next?

Much to my chagrin, I had forgotten to ask what the next steps were. I did not know when to expect to be contacted about the interview and whether it would be by phone or letter. I did not even know who I needed to call to get this critical information. I learned my lesson.

When you go for an interview ensure that you have your questions written down and be prepared to ask them at the end of the interview, when asked if you have any final questions. Ask some of the following:

When might I hear about the results of the interview?

Will I be notified by mail, e-mail, or phone?

Who will be making the call? Will the hiring manager be in contact with me or does the next call from the human resources department?

If I do not hear by the date you suggested, may I call you?

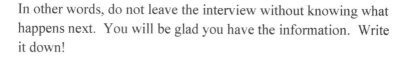

In other words, do not leave the interview without knowing what happens next. You will be glad you have the information. Write it down!

> "Do not leave the interview without knowing what happens next."

Immediately following the interview, after you have collected all the information you need about what happens next, find a quiet place and reflect on what just happened.

Do a self-assessment and ask yourself the following:

How did the interview go?

How did I do? Did I like my answers?

Did I answer all the questions?

If I had it to do over, would I have given the same answers?

Did the interviewer(s) talk more than me?

What do I need to do next time to be better prepared?

Is this where I want to work?

Will this job enable my career strategic plan?

Is this job going to provide me significantly more opportunities than my current position?

Do I have any doubts? If yes, what are they?

Make Yourself Indispensable

You might be surprised by the outcome of this self-assessment. I am convinced it is an essential step after every interview.

Remember, this might be a big move for you and you want to make sure you are making the right decision. There is nothing worse than taking a new job with a new company and after a few weeks realizing you have made a mistake. Maybe the culture is not open to newcomers. Maybe you are not given the computer resources promised. Maybe the work hours are much longer than you were told.

If you can find someone who works at the company that person can be a great resource. You may collect some intelligence about the work atmosphere *before* accepting the position (preferably before the interview). Remember the old adage that "the devil you don't know is worse than the devil you do know."

Thanking Your Interviewer(s)

This is a very important last step of the interview process. Sending a thank-you note is the right thing to do following an interview. My personal opinion is that it should be hand-written and mailed. As an interviewer, I thought that the action that someone would take at the end of the interview cycle was another example of their character. I often would attach the written note to the resume and keep it for future reference.

The thank-you note is also a way that the candidate can remind me of their key qualifications and why he/she is such an ideal candidate for the position. Never miss an opportunity to impress the hiring manager.

Make Yourself Indispensable

KEYS TO INTERVIEW	
Before	Know company and position description Be ready for "what" and "what-if" questions Bring a pen and pad of paper to write things down Be well-dressed and well-rested
During	Use your seven-word brand and PSR vignettes Make eye contact – do not stare Be inquisitive, not precocious (listen more than talk) Know what the next steps are
After	Hand-written thank you note Be politely persistent following up Even if you do not get the job, thank them Do a self-assessment of the interview

At a minimum, you need to send a thank-you note via e-mail. You can also remind the hiring manager of your credentials when doing this. Either way, make sure you say thanks even if you are not selected for the position. You may find a position with the same company at a later date and apply for it. You could find yourself in front of the same recruiter or hiring manager. Do the right thing – say thank you!

Final Negotiations

I believe that if you communicate early and often during the hiring process, the compensation package that you want and deserve will fall into place. But in case you don't believe, let's explore the compensation part of the hiring formula a bit.

Make Yourself Indispensable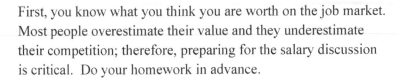

First, you know what you think you are worth on the job market. Most people overestimate their value and they underestimate their competition; therefore, preparing for the salary discussion is critical. Do your homework in advance.

Most job announcements have information on the salary range for a position and you can often use that as a starting point. If you have a friend (maybe the person who referred you to the job in the first place) who works for the company, that person may be able to provide you some ideas about salaries for various positions in the company.

However, salary is only one part of the compensation package. All too often candidates get overly focused on the salary and overlook the rest of the compensation package.

You must consider the bonus structure (most companies have one) and benefits (medical, dental, and life insurance; tuition assistance; travel and buying services; etc.). For example, I know of companies that pay all employee health and medical benefits. That is a significant investment that you need to factor into the compensation conversation.

How about the 401K – what is the company's contribution and when are you "vested" with the company? Do they pay for college tuition and professional certifications? These can be worth tens of thousands of dollars.

> "Salary is only one part of the compensation package."

Make Yourself Indispensable

Despite what companies are likely to tell you, everything is open to negotiation. I once had a hiring manager tell me that my request for more than the standard two weeks of vacation during the first year of employment would have to go to the President of the company for approval.

I said I would help write the memo, if necessary, because I could not sign the offer letter unless I was approved for five weeks of vacation. I got four! Know your boundaries and know your limits but it is more important for you to decide what is important for *you*!

Once you get an offer, think through the options by rehearsing the potential negotiation in reverse order. Start with the package you would like and then think about the likely steps to get there. You will need to determine the most critical benefit for the hiring organization that you can "give" them so that you can offer that concession. (Sebenius, 2004)

I had a very good friend who when negotiating his compensation package asked for two things: high salary and a solid 401K. He asked the prospective employer to give him a final number based on him not taking any benefits, except for the 401K, since he needed no health insurance (he had a private policy), no leave, and no training. All he needed was salary and a 401k; his compensation package was adjusted accordingly.

One final comment about compensation is needed. The package is usually presented and "negotiated" by the most senior person in the human capital shop. Review the final offer very carefully.

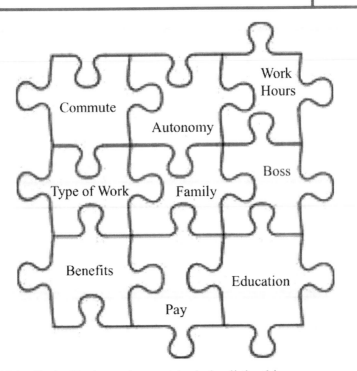

If the final offer letter does not include all the things you negotiated in the conversation such as signing bonus, vacation hours, performance bonus program, severance pay, etc., do not sign the letter until it is correct.

Never sign the letter in the heat of the excitement of receiving the offer. Take a couple of days to reflect on the offer, reflect on the company (is this where you really want to work) and reflect on the position (does it provide you what this entire book talks about – that critical next step in your career progression). Take the time to consider the offer before signing.

Summary

Make Yourself Indispensable

Moving to a new job is hard work. However, if you have worked on your career plan from the very beginning, you know that it will be worth the effort. Start now by reviewing where you are in your career, go back and capture the special learning that you experienced in previous jobs and begin to build your on-line résumé data folder.

It will take some work but take the time today to start the folder and begin building the knowledge base to support your future career aspirations!

Being indispensable and achieving career success are both about deliberate, strategic action. Invest in your career by investing time into networking, your résumé, and interviewing skills.

Make a concerted effort to build your résumé as you build your career; be true to yourself in evaluating your competencies and how you can improve your professional credentials. The more thoughtful you are in how you evaluate yourself and the steps you are taking to improve your competencies, the easier it will be for you to articulate that to others.

You are responsible for your methodical movement toward career success, not anyone else. If you are to land that next job that continues to execute on your career strategy, you are going to have to work for it and not wait for someone to leave the company for you to get a promotion or an opportunity for gaining new job skills.

Make Yourself Indispensable

> "You are responsible for your methodical movement toward career success, not anyone else."

You can never assume that the competition in the job market is going to decrease. Remember that coming up behind you is someone younger with a better, more relevant academic experience who may be more in tune with the latest technology or industry trends.

A good reminder to have above your desk at home, in your notebook binder at work, or on your laptop is the following list of things to do on a monthly basis:

- Networking:

  - Find a reason to communicate with your professional network in some substantive way.
  - Check out job openings in your career field so you know what companies are hiring and the required credentials.
  - Update your LinkedIn profile.

- Résumé Maintenance:

  - Update your on-line résumé data folder.
  - Review and update your résumé, as necessary.
  - Review and update your bio-profile, as necessary.

Make Yourself Indispensable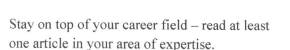

- Stay on top of your career field – read at least one article in your area of expertise.

- At Work:

  - Develop positive habits to improve your communication skills and decision making acumen.
  - Refine your interpersonal skills with your subordinates, peers, and superiors.
  - Refine and execute a career strategy.

Once you decide to pursue a new job, get your résumé distributed to your network, job boards, and recruiters.

Prepare to win your interview by leveraging your communication skills and your compelling résumé.

Do not forget to follow-up and thank your interviewer(s).

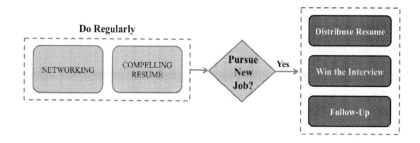

Make Yourself Indispensable

IV. NEVER LOOK BACK...

Passion and persistence trumps everything else in becoming indispensable. Deliberate action related to increasing your core capabilities, enhancing your skills at interacting with others, taking a strategic view of your career, pay-forward networking, and maintaining your compelling résumé are all ways you can differentiate yourself from others.

In each of these dimensions, be balanced: passionate and professional; work hard and play hard; be expert at "what" you do yet attuned as to "how" you do it; and be just as comfortable with high tech tools as you are with high touch approaches.

A one-dimensional professional provides value to fewer organizations than someone with more breadth and depth of competence. In the professional world, if you only have one narrowly focused competence, you are one technological change or minor industry shift away from unemployment. However, even as you are versatile, you must not become a "jack of all trades and master of none."

It is your responsibility to remain relevant in your field and to be an indispensable employee for your current company or an attractive candidate for a new company, if needed.

It is your career! Take responsibility for it and invest early and often into your career. When you finally do make the decision to change jobs and go on interviews ensure that you are not only interesting but also interested!

Make Yourself Indispensable

Success is the result of tailored diligence.

> "Success is the result of tailored diligence."

True success comes from time management and deliberate practice. Do not be afraid to "take out the trash." People appreciate an enthusiastic person doing a simple job much more than an arrogant person doing a complex job.

Do not underestimate the "power of like." Most professionals do not hire or buy from people they do not like.

Stress does not come from working hard; it comes from lack of control. So work hard early in your career so you are calling the shots later.

You do not have to own a company to be in charge of your professional career. However, you must be a solid communicator, astute at interacting with others, and approach your career strategically.

Do not become a "corporate cockroach" - a survivor but not a performer. If your job is to scurry around and stay "busy" but really do little useful then you definitely do not have a vision of your professional identity.[13]

---

[13] This analogy is compliments of Chris Senio, President of Upper Quadrant (2013).

Make Yourself Indispensable

As we close out this book, I have some bad news. There is no "one size fits all" solution to career success. We have suggested that being a job-hopper is bad, yet for some sales jobs changing jobs often actually helps your career.

Similarly, having wide context of the industry or organization that you work in provides insights that prevent you from being ambushed in your dealings. However, there are some people who become very valuable by focusing on one skill, and one skill only. In that situation you had best hope that the demand for that one skill never goes away. Do not be the buggy whip sales person in the 1930's just before automobiles put horse drawn carriages into museums and amusements parks.

Persistence and balance are useful life skills that lead to the qualities needed to become indispensable and achieve career success.

> "There is no "one size fits all" solution to career success. Work hard, continually learn, pay attention to your surroundings, and have balance in all that you do. "

You must work hard and sacrifice early for later gains. The longer you wait to "make your move," the harder it is going to be. In other words, "pay me now or pay me more later." Investing in your future career success is much like investing in a retirement plan – invest early and often.

Start now!

Make Yourself Indispensable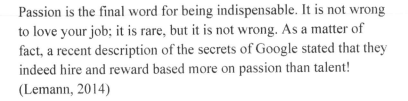

Passion is the final word for being indispensable. It is not wrong to love your job; it is rare, but it is not wrong. As a matter of fact, a recent description of the secrets of Google stated that they indeed hire and reward based more on passion than talent! (Lemann, 2014)

> "Choose a job that you love, and you will never have to work a day in your life."   Confucius

V. REFERENCES

Ankeny, J. (2012, June). The Good Sir Richard. *Entrepreneur*, pp. 30-38.

Begley, S. (2011, January 3). Can You Build a Better Brain? *Newsweek*.

Bergeiesen, M. (2010, October 7). The Neuroscience of Happiness. *SharpBrains, http://www.sharpbrains.com*.

Bossidy, L., & Charan, R. (2002). *Execution: The Discipline of Getting Things Done*. New York: Crown Business Books.

Boufreau, K., Ganglui, I., Gaule, P., Guinan, E., & Lakhani, K. (2012, September 25). Colocation and Scientific Collaboration: Evidence from a Field Experiment. *HBS Working Knowledge*.

Brains Thrive on Challenges. (2012, November 13). *Lumosity Web Site*.

Carnegie Training, Reported on Huffington Post, Pozin, Ilya, 2014, http://www.huffingtonpost.com/2013/07/11/why-people-hate-jobs_n_3579873.html.

Carr, N. (2011). *The Shallows*. New York, NY: WW Norton & Company.

Chemers, M. (1997). *An Integrative Theory of Leadership*. New York: Lawrence Erlbaum Associates.

Cornell, A. W. (1996). *The Power of Focusing.* Oakland, CA: New Harbinger Publications, Inc.

Costa, R. (2012). *Thinking Our Way Out of Extinction.* www.earthsky.org.

Datorres, C. (November 2012). Women, The Key to Success. *FastCompany*, www.FastCompany.com.

Donlea, J. T. (24 June 2011). Inducing Sleep by Remote Control Facilitates Memory Consolidation in Drosphilia. *Science*.

Doucleff, M. (2012, February 11). Anatomy of a Tear Jerker. *Wall Street Journal*.

Duarte, N. (2010). *Resonate - Present Visual Stories That Transform Audiences.* Hoboken, NJ: John Wiley and Sons.

Fernandez, A. (2007, August 22). The Ten Habits of Highly Effective Brains. *Cognitive Neuroscience,Health & Wellness*.

Fisher, C. (23 June 2103). High Brain Integration Underlies Winning Performance of World Class Athletes and Other Top Level Abilities. *Cognition*.

Frederik, P. (2013). "100 Benefits of Meditation" . *www.ineedmotivation.com.*

Gladwell, M. (2008). *Outliers.* New York, NY: Little and Brown Company.

Greenfield, P. (January 2009). Technology and Informal Education: What is Tuaght, What is Learned. *Science*, pp. 69-71.

Habits for Long-term Good Brain Health. (2010, January 10). *Guardian Health Newsletter*.

Hanna, J. (2010, September 20). Power Posing: Fake It Until You Make It. *Harvard Business School, Working Knowledge Newsletter*.

Heskett, J. (2012, July 5). "Why Is Trust So Hard to Achieve in Management?" *Harvard Business School, Working Knowledge Newsletter*.

Heskett, J. (2014, February 4). "Has Listening Become a Lost Art?" *Harvard Business School, Working Knowledge Newsletter*.

House, R. J. (2004). *Culture, Leadership, and Organizations: The GLOBE Study of 62 Societies*. Thousand Oaks: SAGE Publications.

Huckabee, M. (2012). *Dear Chandler, Dear Scarlett*. London: Sentinel.

King, I., & Vangeison, D. (2011). *Overcoming Barriers to Sustainable Innovation and Program Management Within Federal, Aerospace, and Defense Markets*. Chicago, IL: Sopheon.

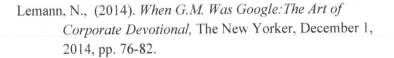

Lemann, N., (2014). *When G.M. Was Google:The Art of Corporate Devotional,* The New Yorker, December 1, 2014, pp. 76-82.

Magretta, J. (2011, December 21). The Most Common Strategy Mistakes. *Harvard Business School, Working Knowledge Newsletter.*

McCullough, David, "Timeless Leadership: A Conversation with David McCullough," Harvard Business Review, pp. 45-49, March 2008.

Miller, G. (1956, Vol 63). The Magical Number Seven, Plus or Minus Two. *The Psychological Review*, pp. 81-97.

Moskowitz, C. (27 April 2008). "Mind's Limit Found: Four Things at Once". *Proceedings of the National Academy of Sciences.*

Neurology, Intense Exercise May Protect Aging Brain. (2011, June 9). *USA Today.*

Nichols, Michael. The Lost Art of Listening. The Guilford Press. NY, NY. 1995.

Nisbett, R. (2003). *The Geography of Thought.* New York, NY: Free Press.

Page, Scott (2011). *The Hidden Factor: Why Thinking Differently is Your Greatest Asset.* Chantilly, VA: The Great Courses.

Penenberg, A. (2011, December). Cognition. *Fast Company.*

Rogers, Carl R. and Roethsliberger, F.J. "Barriers and Gateways to Communication." *Harvard Business Review*, No. 91610 (1991).

Rumelt, R. (2011). *Good Strategy, Bad Strategy.* New York, NY: Crown Business.

Safian, R. (2012). Secrets of the Flux Leader. *Fast Company,* www.FastCompany.com.

Scouller, J. (2011). *The Three Levels of Leadership: How to Develop Your Leadership Presence, Knowhow, and Skill.* Philadelphia: Cirencester: Management Books.

Sebenius, J. (2004, July 26). A Better Way to Negotiate: Backward. *Harvard Business School, Working Knowledge Newsletter.*

Seelig, T. (2009). *What I Wish I Knew When I Was 20.* New York, NY: Harper One.

"Shape Shake-Up". (2012, December). *FastCompany.com,* p. 23.

Sleep is the Best Meditation. http://www.goodreads.com/quotes, (2010).

Sood, A., James, G., Tellis, G., & Zhu, J. (2009). *Predicting the Path of Technological Innovation: SAW Versus Moore, Bass, Gompertz, and Kryder.* Atlanta: Emory University.

Stephens, A. (2013). *Seven Health Benefits of Meditation.* http://foodmatters.tv/articles-1/7-health-benfits-of-meditation.

Strauch, B. (2005). *The Secret Life of the Grownup Brain.* New York, NY: Viking Press.

Suttie, J. (2012, December). Mindfulness and Meditation in Schools for Stress Management. *SharpBrains, http://www.sharpbrains.com.*

Syed, M. (2010). *Bounce.* New York, NY: Harper Collins.

Top 10 Brain Training Future Trends. (2012, August). *SharpBrains, http://www.sharpbrains.com.*

Make Yourself Indispensable

Appendix: Example Résumés and Bio-Profile

Make Yourself Indispensable

Dr. DARREN McKNIGHT   (703) xxx-xxxx
Street Address • City, State Zip Code

"Creating multi-disciplinary solutions to empower enduring productivity"

CAREER OBJECTIVE

Darren is interested in applying his skills and energy in the areas of national security, space safety, sustainable energy, innovation, and education. If you have an organization working in any, or all, of these areas, he would like to speak to you about applying his expertise to improve your organization's productivity and technical excellence immediately and over the long-term.

QUALIFICATIONS SUMMARY

- Darren is an accomplished speaker, scientist, and corporate leader having presented internationally on topics ranging from orbital debris and space insurance to industrial energy and risk management in thirteen countries.
- He strives to constantly learn and teach concepts critical to organizational success: quality decision making, efficient R&D, and effective team dynamics.

EXPERIENCE

INTEGRITY APPLICATIONS INCORPORATED, Chantilly, Virginia
Technical Director, 2010-Present

Darren is responsible for science and technology leadership for space applications and expansion into alternative markets. He develops analytic and comprehensive models to enhance space system survivability. Darren is serving on the Peer Review Working Group of AF Space Command's Astrodynamics Innovation Committee, as a Board Member of the Northern Virginia CTO Roundtable, and was appointed to the International Academy of Astronautics' Committee on Space Debris.

- Advanced understanding of evolution of debris environment through sequence of research papers. Invented concept of Just-in-Time Collision Avoidance (JCA) to address the deficiencies of Active Debris Removal (ADR) to manage the growth of orbital debris cost-effectively.
- Spearheading multi-agency program to create a predictive framework for infectious disease outbreak. Preliminary modeling results produced reliable warnings two weeks before first malaria infection in relation to four key outbreak scenarios.

AGILEX CORPORATION, Chantilly, Virginia
Chief Scientist, 2007-2010

Led activities to exploit advanced technologies, develop proven processes, and apply progressive innovation techniques to a wide variety of customers with a focus on the National Intelligence Community, space sciences, and the renewable energy community for this startup company.

192

- Authored and implemented corporate resource processes essential to establishing new business: Agilex Innovation Methodology (AIM^{SM}), Agilex Interactive Visualization (AIV^{SM}) methodology, and the Agilex Information Surveillance (AIS^{SM}) solution.

SCIENCE APPLICATIONS INTERNATIONAL CORPORATION, McLean, Virginia
Director of Science Technology Strategy, 2004-2007

Darren served as executive for <u>independent research and development (IR&D)</u> and associated thought leadership.

Darren reinvigorated an underperforming IR&D program: tripled the number of proposals submitted and increased IR&D productivity by 60% over two years.

- Invented and implemented corporate innovation process called the Innovation Value Chain. In 2004, Gartner Group selected it as one of the top ten harvestable innovation practices in the world.

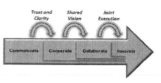

ADDITIONAL EXPERIENCE

CHAIRMAN, BOARD OF ADVISORS, **industrial energy** company ZF Energy Development, 2012-present.

WORKFORCE PRODUCTIVITY CONSULTANT, provide briefs for corporate off-sites, 2009-present.

TITAN CORPORATION, Reston, Virginia, **Senior Vice President for Technology**, 1997-2004. Led chemical/biological remediation technology development programs including the testing and roll-out of a non-ionizing radiation system to sterilize the mail contaminated by *Bacillus anthracis* at the post office in Washington, DC in 2001.

ELECTED **ACADEMICIAN**, INT'L ACADEMY OF ASTRONAUTICS, 1992-Present.

KAMAN SCIENCES CORPORATION, Alexandria, VA, **Principal Scientist**, 1990-1997. Generated $10M in simulation business and authored winning $4M proposal for the first Commercial Space Launch Safety program.

USAF, **Captain**, 1981-1990. At Kirtland AFB, developed analog fiber optic systems at 10% of cost of other sources for EMP testing. As Professor of Physics, USAFA, led the first terrestrial hypervelocity impact test of a satellite.

PUBLICATIONS SUMMARY (List of publications available upon request)

Hitting the Innovation Jackpot, iUniverse, 2011
Soccer is a Thinking Game, iUniverse, 2008
Chem Principles Applied to S/C Ops, Krieger, 1993
Artificial Space Debris, Krieger, 1991
Over 130 articles, papers, patents, trademarks, and presentations

EDUCATION

Ph.D., Aerospace Engineering Sciences, 1986, UNIVERSITY OF COLORADO
M.S., Mechanical Engineering, 1984, UNIVERSITY OF NEW MEXICO
B.S., Engineering Sciences, 1981, UNITED STATES AIR FORCE ACADEMY

Make Yourself Indispensable

LINDA MORRIS

Street Address
City, State Zip Code

Phone: 703.xxx.xxxx
Email: Linda.xxxx@veriz.com

QUALIFICATIONS SUMMARY:
I am an enthusiastic and inventive leader motivated by change.

EDUCATION: *Building a foundation for a career in diplomacy*

James Madison University-Rising Junior - Major:International Affairs – Minor: Italian
Paul VI Catholic High School – 2011 – graduated with a 3.74 cumulative GPA

WORK EXPERIENCE: *Looking for challenges...*

Sales Associate, Athleta   2011-2013
Athleta was an online company for 10 years before deciding to go to brick and mortar. I
was part of the team that opened our third store on the east coast. I learned about
teamwork and communication as well as dealing with difficult people and unforeseen
problems.

Assistant Swim Coach, International Country Club   2013
International Country Club had not had a winning team in years. I was brought in to
foster team spirit and improve team performance. We have been winning because of
techniques taught in practice and team spirit I have fostered. I am in charge of 108
children, ages 4-18, every day.

Assistant Swim Coach, Oakton Swim and Racquet Club   2009-2012
PUPs Director, Oakton Swim and Racquet Club   2011-2012
Oakton Swim and Racquet Club saw a need for a program for the 3 and 4 year olds who
were not old enough to be on the swim team, but still wanted to be a part of the team. I
facilitated a swim program for those swimmers and helped get them involved in the team.

Coach, Swim with Beth Program   2012
I was hired by a family friend to help coach 4-7 year olds in her winter swim program. I
focused on basic swim skills and instilling confidence in the water.

LEADERSHIP: *Quickly assimilated into communities with focus on integrity...*

My work experience has taught me how to communicate effectively with people and
resolve conflict resolution; this has translated in to leadership opportunities in my
schooling.

James Madison University Honor Council
James Madison University Student Government Representative (Junior Class)
Kappa Alpha Theta-Philanthropy Committee
Paul VI Catholic School Student Body President

194

Make Yourself Indispensable

Roger Campbell, ACC

Management Consultant/Executive Coach
xxxx@verizon.com
703 xxx-xxxx

Mr. Campbell brings over 35 years of experience as a management consultant, executive coach and subject matter expert in human capital and talent management. He has successfully supported major change initiatives in all areas of human capital and is widely recognized for his vision, coaching and strategic planning expertise. His unique blend of public and private sector experience delivers great value and perspective to his clients.

Coaching Approach

Mr. Campbell's coaching focuses on moving his clients forward, challenging his clients to accept only successful outcomes and to celebrate those successes. Mr. Campbell works with leaders to clarify their situation and to identify next steps, with a focus on career strategies, work and personal roadblocks, and leadership challenges. He has extensive experience working with teams and leaders to identify strategies and opportunities to build a stronger organization and improve the bottom line. He works closely with executives needing help in their transition to new opportunities and with leaders in the military service seeking to transfer their skills and competencies to the private sector. Mr. Campbell has a proven track record of assisting executives in transition. He is considered by many to be an expert in résumé construction, interviewing techniques and networking.

Experience

Mr. Campbell has served for the last twelve years as a senior consultant and advisor for some of the best and most respected consulting firms in the country. He is the former Chief Human Capital Officer for a large intelligence organization and has held senior positions in human capital in large private sector firms. He served as the Director of Government Consulting Services for Monster.com and has worked as a senior consultant/subject matter expert in support of multiple initiatives in the federal sector. He has published articles and has led webcasts on topics associated with human capital challenges in the both the public and private sector. Mr. Campbell's extensive experience provides the background for the often much needed support that busy executives and emerging leaders and their teams need to continue their move to the next level of performance.

Mr. Campbell is actively engaged in volunteer activities with local charities in support of the unemployed. He is often called upon to provide seminars to a variety of clients. He serves as an adjunct professor at Georgetown University and at his alma mater, George Mason University. He is a certified facilitator and has helped organizations develop and implement their strategic plan. He is certified on various assessment instruments including the MBTI, Hogan, Voices 360, and the DDI Leadership Mirror.

Make Yourself Indispensable

Security Clearance
> Active clearances held

Previous Clients

> Senior Executives and Emerging Leaders in the Public Sector
> C level leaders in small to mid-size companies

Professional Highlights

> Advisor, Center for Human Capital Innovation
> Member, Talent Board, Human Capital Institute
> Founder, Campbell Consulting Solutions

Education

> BS in Business Administration, George Mason University
> Certificate in Leadership Coaching, Georgetown University
> Certified Facilitator
> Leadership Training, Federal Executive Institute, Harvard University, Leadership for Senior Executives

45662547R00110

Made in the USA
Middletown, DE
10 July 2017